Still Point-Life Notes From A Kentucky Woman

A Coal Camp

By

Sarah Cornett Hagen

Kentucky Coal Poet

Sarah L Cornett Hagen

2010

authorHOUSE™

1663 Liberty Drive, Suite 200
Bloomington, Indiana 47403
(800) 839-8640
www.AuthorHouse.com

This book is a work of non-fiction. Names of people and places have not been changed to protect their privacy.

First published by AuthorHouse 04/12/2010

ISBN: 978-1-4184-9053-9 (sc)

Library of Congress Control Number: 2004096096

Printed in the United States of America
Bloomington, Indiana

This book is printed on acid-free paper.

Cover Art by Asha
www.ashaart.com
Ph 541-973-7497

DEDICATION

To my hardy, everlasting ancestral tree with my small family branch firmly attached - my son Brett, my daughter Laura, my granddaughters - Regena, Lydia and my newly born "Ides of March" Great-niece,

Arwen Raine Sergent, who was blessed to be born
beneath the shadow of Pine Mountain.

AND

My dear "Mate" Warren, who has managed the home front and kept my coffee cup filled for so many years while I have roamed the fields of daisies in my mind- for his patient ear and ever present quiet support-

I am forever grateful.

Thank you.

Haymond, Kentucky

TABLE OF CONTENTS

WAKING UP IN A COAL CAMP **1**

THE BATH HOUSE **5**

FIGHTING THE ENEMY **11**

GRANDMA'S HOUSE **13**
GRANDMA'S STOVE 14
DAILY LIFE AT GRANDMAS 14

HAYMOND SOCIETY **19**
LIFE ON THE RAILROAD TRACK 19
THE ROW HOUSES 20
FRONT PORCHES 21
BACK PORCHES 23

GRANDMA'S MORAL VALUES **27**

GRANDMA'S STORIES **33**
GRANDMA'S SUPPER 33
GRANDMA'S FISHING DAYS ON SOUTH FORK OF THE POUND RIVER 43

THE TIPPLE PLAYGROUND **51**

HAYMOND GRADE SCHOOL **55**

UNCLE FRED KINCER **57**

HEALTH AND WELFARE **59**
DOCTORING 59
DISASTERS AND CALAMITIES 61
HOME CARE 63
SANITATION 65

THE HAYMOND COMPLEX **67**
THE SHOW HALL 67
THE POOL HALL 68
THE FOUNTAIN 68
THE POST OFFICE 68

THE COMPANY STORE **71**

LIVING IN A CAMP HOUSE **73**

FAMILY RITUALS **77**
WASH NIGHT 77
BATH NIGHT 78

CHANGING TIMES **81**

SURVIVAL **83**

TRADITIONS **85**
QUILTING, WEAVING, DARNING, KNITTING AND SHUCKY BEANS 85
…AND SHUCKY BEANS… 87

LEGACY **93**
DADDY'S BANJO 93
DADDY'S DAUGHTER 99
LET ME 101

ACKNOWLEDGMENTS

No writer writes alone.

Ally Dellemare has been my incredible gift as a friend, mentor, editor and artist for my work. Her belief in my words and her gentle, persistent guidance brought my book to fruition.

I thank everyone who has kept my writer's pen filled with their stories and offered me the encouragement to keep writing. I have a long list of readers with whom I have shared my work through the years. I especially want to thank my Berea sisters, Artricia Campbell Gordon and Dorothy May Todd, for their continuing interest and critiquing of my book.

FOREWORD

My heart, overflowing with my Kentucky memories, keeps me placed. I am a woman from a world where women's dreams were pinned to a clothesline or melted by the fiery heat of a cook stove.

November 1, 2000

Snow has once again whitened the mountains far above us. The saddle I can see in the distant mountain is white-the air is crisp and not too cold. Spent, bright autumn leaves are falling madly into the cold of winter. Rain fell last night in the valley but it was still a surprise to see how low the snow line is this morning.

Still Point is gently being wooed into winter. It has taken me years to accept Still Point as my home. An unrelenting battle has waged within me to accept Oregon and etch my heart with the land marks of southern Oregon. Who would not want to claim such natural grandeur as their own? But I know my ancestors never walked or tilled this land. They never loved, gave birth or their blood, sweat and tears to claim this world. These mountains hold no familiar places for yesterday's child who lives inside me, neither babbling brooks nor mossy glens where my childhood secrets are stored away.

The pungent smell of coal rising from the hollows mixed with the exotic perfume of wild honeysuckle and mountain laurel nectar is my lost elixir. Chewing the sweetness of birch bark, tasting wild persimmons and wild strawberries, and quenching my thirst from a mountain spring all were mine. Now, forever lost..... Forever Lost.

I often wonder where I would be
if I had not wondered about things around me.

Wondering, as a child at play,
how the sky and stars were made.
How did clouds know when to rain?
How did plants learn to drink with their feet?
How did a bird know how to build a nest?
or what to feed its helpless young, dried seeds or earthworms?
Why did countries go to war?
to take the men who would live no more?
Why did love turn to hate,
when fickle hearts sought to escape?
How would I, the woman I would become,
sort out this world and find a place for me?

Dawning of my understanding occurred. I realized the band of time was growing narrower and the years were melting away. I knew it was time for me to tentatively claim this valley and mountains around me as my home. Oregon soil is no different than the earth my spirit longs for in my memory. The key is my acceptance of my life as I have lived it. We are cast into the winds of time and eventually root somewhere and have our life harvest. Lonely and empty is the heart denied this experience that claims no home; a bereft, floating entity attached to no one and no place.

I have always known I was born indelibly stamped as a "child of nature." This child grew into a "hearth and home woman" whose heart affairs carried her to foreign places with the "child of nature" living quietly inside. This hallowed gift I have carried with me like so many carefully wrapped seeds from home is waiting to be planted and nurtured. My heart, my memories, my life brought to this sanctuary, Still Point.

Perhaps after you read this book you will embrace the richness of the soil of my mountain heritage where this "child of nature" first took root. The highland traditions passed down to me from past generations of strong, resilient women solidly resolved to combat life. The honest hardworking men, who shortened their lives digging for the black gold, who became their husbands. This is the powerful heritage I am made from. I proudly and humbly share my gift with you my reader.

The Author as a child

WHEN A LITTLE GIRL DREAMS

When a Little Girl dreams
the world is filled with goodness and light.
The morning star and evening star guide her way,
as her bare feet make prints in dew-dropped paths of knee high grass.
The raucous cry of a crow fills the air
as he keeps his eye on the field of maturing sweet corn.
The gentle sound of the clucking hen calling her baby chicks-
All happens when a Little Girl dreams.
When a Little Girl dreams,
sun-splashed days appear and shade trees gently sway.
Fireflies light her evening sky, pollywogs in the pond multiply.
Butterflies, yellow and gold, come and sit on her shoulders,
When a Little Girl dreams
the garden rows become her friends-
waving their headdresses, frilly carrot tops to tasseling corn,
The mistress spider spins and weaves gauzy threads,
Reflecting sunbeams and moonbeams in her web.
When a Little Girl dreams,
She has much to learn about this life,
So dream , Sweet Child, dream.

PROLOGUE

The phone rings one late afternoon at Still Point. It is my brother, Albert, with a message my heart did not want to hear.

To The Mountain Eagle:

As you work your way along the backbone of the Cumberlands, headed toward your lofty home on Pine Mountain, please cast a caring eye down the valley toward Pine Creek. The dark shadow you see hovering along the creek bank beneath the rising mist is covering the homeplace of Aunt Normie. The light of Aunt Normie is dimmed forever. My Aunt Normie is gone. She is my last direct link to my Kentucky roots. There could be no finer goodbye than for me to proudly proclaim my right to Aunt Normie and her life on Pine Creek. It is difficult to imagine in today's fast-paced world that you can live and act out all the emotions of your given days with such peace and understanding as Aunt Normie did. My aunt lost several children to childhood diseases. Mary Lois, I especially remember as the child of ten who after years of suffering finally succumbed to leukemia when I was in high school.

Aunt Normie prized her kitchen and cellar and she kept her basement shelves filled with canned goods from her vegetable garden and her kitchen rich with smells of constant food preparations...could be fried chicken and biscuits for supper or wild huckleberries from the big mountain being made into jam for winter.

I am the eldest child from a family of five. We were nieces and nephews to our Aunt Normie who already had her own measure of family to claim. She always made room for her younger brother, (Garnard) and his family. I can remember my very early days when my family went visiting on Pine

Creek. The minute you rounded the bend at the Old Regular Baptist Church at Mayking and crossed over the bridge you could see the beginning of the road going up Pine Creek. The road was roughly etched out on the hillside and dropped sharply to follow the natural path made by the creek. I could sense Daddy's reaction to paying a home visit. We would slowly inch our way up the rutted dirt road. Daddy would start waving to people, calling everyone aunt or uncle until eventually the inevitable would happen. Daddy would bring the car to a halt as I could see someone headed toward us. "OH LORD, please don't let him see me," this shy child prayed. The back seat was my safe haven and I hoped nobody would notice me.... maybe I was invisible. The conversation would torturously wind its way toward me. Daddy would slowly roll the window down further and lean forward resting his chest against the steering wheel.

A wizened face would peer in and give me close scrutiny. "I declare, she is a fine looking young'un, Garnard." A sense of belonging flooded over me even though I would be too overwhelmed to tell my name.

Trips to Pine Creek were few and special. Our visits were planned around the seasons and childbirth. The road to Aunt Normie's was pockmarked with chug holes and exposed rocks. The chug holes became giant teacups that held the seasonal brews. Wintertime, the depressions were frozen solid with a snow topping and the spring thaws turned the winter dessert into a molasses colored mud. During the summer months the cups were replenished by thunderheads that were spawned on the big mountain. Finally, the brief autumn dried up the pits and dust filled the holes–the best time to travel up Pine Creek.

Aunt Normie's mother was my Grandma Kincer (Ollie Craft). She kept close ties to Pine Creek in my early childhood and teen-hood. We lived in Haymond and it seemed she was always going to Pine Creek. "Word" would be sent to her when she was needed because telephones were scarce in our world, but families suffering from sickness or death would find her. My cousins and I thought she enjoyed going to funerals as she was always ready to stay with some grieving family and the long vigilant nights of "sitting up" with the deceased. When we innocently brought this fact to her attention I can still see my grandmother laugh and, of course, we children never understood the joke.

Time has a way of softening our losses. I remember the time Daddy insisted we take a trip to Pine Creek which was always hard to fit in my busy schedule. I was home on one of my hurried visits as I had always lived "far-off" as an adult. The time frame was the late sixties. This trip he also took me to Cram Creek where his maternal grandparents had lived. For the first time I saw their homeplace where my father had spent his childhood. My grandfather had died a painful death at an early age(33)of Brights Disease so Grandma Kincer had to rely on her family to help raise her orphaned children. The memories had been too painful for Daddy to share until now. He told me about following the horse drawn wagon on foot from Cram Creek to the cemetery on Pine Creek.

Suddenly, I am making the pilgrimage to Pine Creek as a grieving widow. Mother is at my side and we are paying a visit to Aunt Normie. I am shocked to see Grandma Kincer appear at the door. "I know," Aunt Normie says, "Everybody tells me I look just like Mommy." A familiar longing hit me and a deep peace swept over me.

The years moved swiftly and I returned to Aunt Normie's doorstep every chance I possibly could. She would bring down her priceless quilts from the attic for me to view. "Charlene, bring down the Flower Garden," she would say. Charlene would appear with heaps of the latest quilts Aunt Normie had made. (Charlene, her child who had suffered lifelong tragic effects from measles leaving her forever with my Aunt Normie.)

One later visit, my Mother and I found Aunt Normie gardening her beautiful flower beds from her wheel chair. Life had changed dramatically since Aunt Normie had been widowed. She had taken many senior citizen trips and she found a new life at the Center where the ladies met and did their quilts. Her grandchildren were blossoming in great profusion and the grandchildren were requesting her honored presence at their nuptials.

My last visit with Aunt Normie was in April 1995, the Tuesday following Easter Sunday. The Kentucky hills were bursting with spring bloom. The forsythia, dogwood and redbud were echoing the renewal of the earth and the house finches had reclaimed their home over Aunt Normie's back door. Something I had always distinctly remembered because the birds nested so close you could reach up and touch the nest. Her dining room table was still dressed in lace from the Easter Sunday dinner. "Yes, some of the children were here for dinner on Sunday" she said, "I declare, I can't cook like I use to." The phone rang several times and the mailman had a special package to deliver. I watched in amazement as I saw the world come to her door. The afternoon wore on as my mother and I were caught up in Aunt Normie's world. The photograph albums came to life with people known and unknown. Newspaper clippings fell out from unexpected places. I saw names, events from my family recorded and lovingly stashed away. I knew then that anyone who crossed the threshold of Aunt Normie's home was a part of Pine Creek. I saw the album she had kept of the Center with every quilt made, its owner, the completion date and the picture of the quilt and the creator. Aunt Normie was a living historian!

Her gift as an artisan is in the legacy of her quilts. The exquisite handiwork and range of colors were from her palette. Her works can never be repeated. My Aunt Normie, Norma Craft, the Lady, who lived on Pine Creek. Tap roots from a mountain heritage run deep. Tendrils of these roots are wrapped gently around my heart forever.

Sarah Lydia (Kincer) Cornett-Hagen

STILLPOINT

Ashland, Oregon

November 11, 1995

Garnard (Sarah's Father), Aunt Normie,
Aunt Vestie, Uncle Joe and Grandma Kincer

WAKING UP IN A COAL CAMP

The shouting silence fills my ears with its quietness, almost as intense as the cloying, sweet smell of the honeysuckle perfume wafting over my body. One weighted moment of empty air, real as a note on a guitar, sets my ears ringing, before the incessant roaring hum begins.

Thus starts a new day in Haymond, Kentucky, the Heart of Coal Mining Country.

The mechanical giant that governs our lives declares the opening of another day with the noise of an awakened dinosaur. A gigantic creak followed by a loud moan, then the thunderous sound of shuddering gears, shifting and turning, leaving the earth trembling from the vibration--the tipple starts to run. The tipple operation is where coal is mechanically graded into uniform pieces after the long ride down the mountain side in the open-air wooden chute and then "coal gons" are loaded from the oversized funnel hanging over the railroad track.

I was born one sultry August afternoon in 1936 within the sight and sound of this scene.

The sleeping house responds with a slight tremor as the steady hum enters into my distant dreams and I become aware of my bed mate cousins. My body has finally made peace with the thrashing army of limbs and my eyes are heavy with sleep. I can feel the cool morning air sucking up the stifling heat leftover from yesterday's scorching day.

The din from the tipple is the wake-up call for the townspeople. The sound courses through their blood bringing them old thoughts for the new day, the sameness never ends. The bedroom curtains reply by moving slightly in the early morning light.

Startup of the tipple stirs the settled coal dust and I can taste the oily residue on my tongue. My first conscious breath inhales the odor of coal with its pure, earthy smell. My groggy senses tell me coal is a bounty from nature, black as night from being stored in the earth for eons. Coal has a pungent, mossy smell when taken fresh from the earth. This scent changes to the heavy smell of hot tar at the tipple site. Black tar was used to glue our narrow roads into a smooth path and this same blackness, in searing summer heat, would ooze through layers of gravel in the roadbed, stick to your bare feet OR ruin your good Sunday shoes.

Every mining community was painted a coded color by the company. Our camp town was all white with black trim but it never showed white because of the coating of grime. The instant the tipple started meant stirring up the coal dust which settled like a black shroud over the camp. The "row houses" nearest the tipple suffered most from this problem and my grandmother's house was in this row, only a few hundred yards from the tipple. The houses were permanently tinged with a black coat, making the gray days seem grayer and sunlight dimmer on clear days. When the frequent lightning-filled summer storms occurred the town was given a good rinsing and briefly sparkled. The camp returned ever so quickly to a dull state of tarnished grayness, the brief period of brightness went unnoticed.

Children were left in their beds until the morning rush was past. The murmur of voices, the smell of coffee brewing, eggs, sausage and bacon frying were woven into early morning dreams. Grandma Kincer was busy at work turning out her pans of biscuits and putting the finishing touches on the big iron skillet of sausage gravy to be ladled over her hot biscuits.

No boarder went to bed hungry nor any miner, lifting the lid on his dinner bucket she had fixed before he made it to the top of the mountain.

Five-thirty in the morning speaks the time of day the day shift starts trudging toward the mine talking quietly and taking a draw on their first cigarette of the day. An occasional hacking cough would break the morning reverie. The graveyard shift of miners filed wearily past the morning shift outside the mine and waited their turn to ride the dolly down the mountainside. This open-bedded vehicle ran on a small track powered by a giant pulley operated from the mine on top of the mountain.

The exhausted men of the night shift carried an empty dinner bucket and their jacket in one hand, held a gratifying cigarette in the other. Their clothes stiff with dried mud and coal dust cemented together by their sweat. The blackened faces with red-rimmed eyes, laughed in unison over the latest joke told on the job that night. The night workers had the prospects of an unbearably hot day ahead to be restored by sleep. First stop would be at my grandmothers.

Grandma's House

THE BATH HOUSE

The bathhouse was a rough unpainted structure built off to the right side of the boardinghouse. The building sat far enough into the backyard to give a sense of privacy and separation from the big house. A wooden walkway, built close to the boardinghouse, went directly from the street to the bathhouse. The inside walls of the bathhouse were lined with wooden lockers on two sides placed high enough to allow a row of pegs underneath to hold the miners outer garments. The lockers had numbers painted on the padlocked doors and held a change of clothes and personal items for the miner. Two long benches were positioned beneath the lockers placed slightly away from the wall so the lockers could be accessed. A small heating stove sat on a raised hearth in the middle of the room. Hot water was piped in from the mammoth storage tank behind the coal fed kitchen range in grandma's kitchen. An open shower pit filled one corner of the building on the left hand side of the room. The square of concrete floor flanged up the sides about a foot so you had to step into the shower box. A half wall ran down the side nearest the outside door for privacy but the front of the shower box was open. The back wall of the shower sported two showerheads with leaky, rusting pot metal handles which spouted forth water when the handles were turned on. The miners would soap down and sit on the "waiting bench" inside the shower pit and wait their turn to rinse off. Sheets of linoleum lined the shower walls. The linoleum, cracked and peeling from the constant moisture, allowed water to seep through and saturate the inside wall giving the bathhouse a dank, pervasive smell. This odor was intensified by roaring fires in the wintertime and a repugnant smell to young girls of miner's sweat mingled with shaving cream, shaving lotion, soap and stale tobacco. Faded, thick linoleum covered the creaky floor. One tiny window on the wall, which connected the shower pit to the lockers, was draped with heavy burlap. No peeping tom or natural light was allowed to enter. Another window on the opposite wall was open for ventilation in the summer months. This window was higher, high enough to discourage curious eyes and gave some relief to the sweltering miners inside. These windows were painted black to insure further privacy. Two sixty-watt bare light bulbs, evenly spaced, hung over the benches burned constantly casting an eerie half-life glow in the dark room. Eyes had to adjust to the gloomy light regardless of the season.

My cousin Agnes (Aggie), reminded me of an incident that happened when we were quite young. One of Grandma's star boarders, Rural Vaughan, had a visit from his son who was on leave from the army. It seems the young man ran out of soap and Cousin Aggie was sent to the bathhouse with a new bar. She handed the soap through the cracked door and, in return, found something placed in her hand that sent her racing back to the house to tell our grandma. "Boy, did she put the skits under him in a hurry," my cousin recalls. I have been in close contact with my dear cousins, Eva Dean and Agnes Lenora, who are sisters. They are adding more detail to the painting of our growing up days in a coal mining camp while weaving a renewed web of family ties that bind us together in cousin history. We grew up in such exciting times. I have much to share with you, my readers. Our grandma would be proud knowing I told you about our lost world lived in the mountains.

The bathhouse was a social center for the camp. The double houses had no bathrooms so grandma made extra money running a public bathhouse. Grandma charged ten cents for the luxury of taking a shower and the bather provided his own soap and towel. Working miners were charged two dollars a month and this included his family as well. Grandma's boarders had this privilege included in their room and board. Electricity and water were free utilities when Elkhorn Consolidated Coal Company began their operation but later charged the disgruntled miners two dollars a month which was taken out of their monthly check. Meanwhile, the miner's family would run up a high bill "trading" at the commissary so little money was left for the miner to claim as his own.

Our legendary two-gun toting sheriff, Willard Hall, was a watchdog for the coal company in the days of free utilities. He was known to keep the town law-abiding by shooting out front porch lights of offenders disobeying the 8 AM, "lights out" rule, so it was told. This action helped remind people to watch their excessive abuse of electricity. We children were terrified by the sight of the sheriff with his uniform and guns holstered to his sides and avoided him whenever possible.

In later years, electricity was provided by Bluegrass companies which eased the responsibilities of the local law. However, providing the town with good water is a problem to this day. My uncle Lank and his buddy, Fred, bought the water rights to the town of Haymond years after the Big Mine folded. The antiquated system brought many headaches to the new owners. The two fold problem-constant repair to the water lines and customers slow to pay the $3.50 monthly fee-gave them little capital to work with. The community, not able to depend on the water flow, gave them further excuse to not pay their water bill. AND money was scarce. The town could find itself going days without water. The new promise is the town will be linked to an updated water system with neighboring towns to solve the problem.

The water system I remember during my high school years gushed rust-red, rotten egg smelly water into your kitchen sink, bathtub or washing machine. This was a vile liquid, which would ruin your favorite white outfit if the water had been shut off for a period of time to repair water lines. Iron rust you cannot remove from fabric or appliances. Orange red rust permanently marked the kitchen sink and bathroom fixtures in a coal camp. Sadly, a problem created by mining the coal. Our pure mountain streams and plentiful water supply has been forever tainted by mining run-off, the disturbed minerals of iron and sulfur.

In later years, after the Big Mine shut down, the bathhouse was used by the family. Bathrooms were slow in coming to the mining town of Haymond so the bathhouse remained a prominent fixture in our everyday lives. My cousin Aggie and I used to shower and dress in the bathhouse before heading down to the Fountain (part of the complex of the post office/theater/recreation hall) or, if we were REALLY LUCKY, maybe given a chance go to a movie at Jenkins or Neon. Nothing could be more exciting than getting ready for a football game on a cool autumn night in the bathhouse while you could hear cars screeching up and down the road, honking their horns and cheering, revving up for the big game rivalry with Whitesburg, the county seat. Later, arriving at the game knowing you looked just right, was the ultimate thrill. I'm not sure this euphoria had any affect on the outcome of the game but we felt the team could not have survived without us.

Sarah,Agnes and friend Frances

FIGHTING THE ENEMY

Fighting coal dust was a useless battle the women waged. To stay clean was impossible with the continuous supply of coal dust emanating from the tipple. Coal buckets kept a steady tracking of coal dust from the coal house to the inside. Every time the stove was loaded, a fine spray of coal dust would settle around the stove to be swept up. Sweeping the dust would cause it to settle on the furniture and walls creating the endless cycle. House cleaning was difficult work and spring cleaning anticipated with determination to win the battle. The brief summer months were enjoyed with coats of new paint, fresh wall paper and no fires built in the stoves.

Coal dust is not ordinary topsoil dust, but an industrial strength coating consisting of mica-sized particles of coal which blackens the world around the people who unearth it. Coal dust can only be removed by a caustic cleaner such as lye soap. The women faithfully scrubbed down the front walls and porches of their homes which invariably turned their hands into rawhide. The introduction of detergents in the forties was the saving grace for coal camps. Oxydol was the choice laundry soap at my house but the "Tide's In and Dirt's Out" jingle from Proctor Gamble was sung most often on wash days. The company, headquartered in Cincinnati, across the Ohio River, must have made billions of dollars sudsing down their neighbor, eastern Kentucky.

Housecleaning was a competitive art among the women as they daily tackled the enemy. Everyone knew Rove Trent to be the finest housekeeper in our row. Although she lived near the tipple she managed to wear the royal crown, her windows filled with glass shelves of whatnots and covered with Venetian blinds always sparkled. The last conversation I had with her she was sitting in her porch swing, mourning the death of my father. "I shore miss Garnard,"she says looking at me misty-eyed, "he always kidded me I would kill myself working so hard fighting this ole coal dust. Now he's gone before me and I'm still fighting it."

"Sleep tight, don't let the bedbugs bite," the old saying goes. Kids with red-speckled legs racing down the stairs in the morning meant another familiar enemy had returned. All the beds had to broken down and sprayed for bedbugs. Every crevice in the bed frame, seams and buttons on the mattresses, coils in the bedsprings checked and a hearty dose of spray given. Another tedious backbreaking chore to be added to housekeeping duties!

GRANDMA'S HOUSE

Grandma Kincer at Haymond house

GRANDMA'S STOVE

Grandma had running water in her kitchen which was special as few homes had this convenience. Hot water was available as long as the firebox of the huge kitchen range was kept filled with coal to heat the enormous water tank behind the stove. This was a massive commercial-sized cast iron stove, heavily decorated with ornate silver-colored metal gingerbread. The stove occupied the entire end of the room and stood high. My cousin, Aggie, remembers the oven door was strong enough to stand on and certainly too heavy to be opened by us children. There would be no chance to peek at the goodies baking inside that oven in grandma's kitchen. When the stove was in use the heat was fierce and it became a monster belching boiling water in its back tank and voraciously eating coal.

We were cautioned to stay away from that end of the kitchen and ONE DAY we were made true believers. Poor Ivan, one of grandma's longtime boarders, was struck by a spell of "saint vitus dance" when he was stoking the fire. He lifted the stove lid and suddenly thrust his poker-stiff hands into the fire and the fire crept up his arms until it engulfed his body. The nervous condition gives the victim super human strength and no one could pull his arms out in time to save him. Poor Ivan was hospitalized and died shortly afterwards from the horrible burns.

DAILY LIFE AT GRANDMAS

A Maytag washer hugged the back porch wall when not in use. The machine was rolled into the kitchen in the wintertime and clothes hung on the backyard clothesline or back porch. In bad weather the kitchen became a drying room. The outhouse backed up against the hill, far away from the house as possible. Electricity, "juice", was available in single 60-watt bulbs fed by a skinny black cord running up the side wall and tacked to the middle of the ceiling. The humble chandelier swung freely and rolls of tacked fly tape curled loosely from the ceiling ready to trap houseflies and insects attracted to the light. Fly tape was one of the first everyday poisons introduced for home use. No one questioned why the insects were attracted to the sticky tape and an instant death. Slowly and surely we innocently began poisoning our world.

The ice man, Charley Tolliver, came twice a week in the summer, less often in the winter to deliver blocks of ice for the ice box. He made a good living supplying ice to the mining communities before refrigerators. An exciting ritual we kids enjoyed was eating ice chips he would give us as we clustered around the ice truck. Creamy ice cream could not have competed with the cooling flavor of pure water frozen into ice on a hot summer day. A favorite sneaky thing for cousins to do was stick our finger into a naked electric socket hidden behind the ice box, for the thrilling jolt of being shocked. Warnings from our elders made the forbidden more exciting. Timid me was always the last one to try it.

My widowed grandmother did not have an easy life supporting her family running a boardinghouse and in later years was rewarded with a passel of grandchildren constantly underfoot. She ran her life with her peace button in place, never raising her voice or becoming impatient with her rambunctious grandchildren.

Grandma kept a flock of chickens in a chicken yard on the hillside belonging to Uncle Fred. From her, I learned the secrets of chicken innards as I watched her deftly dissect a hen into a wishbone, four legs, and peel out the pale yellow inner lining of the highly prized bluish-purple gizzard, full of fine grit. She never seemed to mind my morbid interest in the chicken's internal organs as I would pepper her with questions to satisfy my insatiable curiosity.

Hens were carefully monitored by her to determine when their laying cycle permanently ended. They would be earmarked for a Sunday dinner of chicken and dumplings before they became tough old birds. Occasionally a mistake was made and a hen would have an egg sack full of yolks in various stages of development, from tiny yellow specks to full-sized yolks, ready for the shell. Grandma would break the egg sack loose and add it the simmering broth, sad about killing a laying chicken, but "allowing's how the flavor of the dumplings would be mighty fine."

A summer season in Kentucky was never complete without lining shelves in the smokehouse, cellar or backroom with jars of apple butter, blackberry and strawberry jam and apple, blackberry and grape jelly. Your grandma was nearby whether you lived in a camp row house or farm house ready to teach you how to cook, can, and preserve food. You felt cooking was an art that flowed naturally through your veins. "The better cook you are, the better feller you will catch," if you believed the implications Grandma Kincer made and no granddaughter wants to disappoint her grandmother.

Grandma had two trees in her side yard. The tree nearest the sidewalk was a huge leafy sycamore which shed its leaves constantly after they turned yellow and curled into balls of hopelessness. No doubt, pollution from the mining operation kept the tree anemic. Grass would not grow either which further verified a pollution hazard. We children played happily in the dirt yard and would sweep the yard under grandma's instructions to keep the yard free of loose dirt. The yard was hard as cement and gave us plenty of room to jump rope and play house. The apple tree sat further back in the yard nearer the bathhouse and seemed unaffected by the pollution. The tree behaved as if its sole purpose was to produce sour, tangy apples every year, which our grandma turned into her famous fried apple pies. Grandma always had a few rows of tomatoes, beans and corn planted in her back yard, plus a lettuce and onion bed made of dirt fine as silk. The garden was hidden behind a row of elephant-eared, fleshy red-stalked rhubarb plants that stretched the width of her backyard. In front of the rhubarb was her flower bed ablaze with orange-red canna lilies and sunflowers. I know this was hard work for her but now, when I think about it, I realize that gardening probably took her back to Pine creek and the gardens of her youth.

HAYMOND SOCIETY

LIFE ON THE RAILROAD TRACK

The front "row houses" were built a hair's breath from the highway. Further down below our row the town spread out to include The Back Alley, consisting of small three room houses built where the valley was wider. Bear Holler, located behind the town complex of the fountain, post office, pool hall and theater, held a row of double houses you could see from the school house hill. The valley is but a sliver of flatland, and Elkhorn Coal Company crowded this strip of valley floor with the rudiments of town living. The houses were built precariously close to the highway, only a narrow band of sidewalk and a dirt strip separated the houses from the road. The ribbon of daily living which bound the people together was the front porches, the sidewalks and the highway, edged by narrow creek on the other side. Above the creek, on the hillside ran the railroad track leading to the tipple. The railroad yard near the tipple was jammed with coal gons. The empties were lined up on the back track ready to be filled at the tipple while the front track carried the coal out of our hills.

A dangerous separate life was lived on the railroad tracks and one that led to "no good". This is where serious card games were played by the gambling men of the camp and bootleg moonshine whiskey enjoyed. A young man could test his mettle in this circle of hardened men, keeping his shenanigans secret lest his family found out. Knife fights and fist fights were the usual methods of settling scores and it was a well known secret who could throw the heaviest punch or quick draw his knife the fastest.

THE ROW HOUSES

There were no front yards to divide the houses, just a continuous line of double houses with a coal house between the two buildings. The front porch was the connector of coal camp living. A middle banister divided the front porch into two separate porches which meant you could cross the banister be on your neighbor's porch, go down their front steps, walk around a coal house shared by two families and be at the front steps of the next house. Wooden platforms, with communal free-standing water spigots, were evenly spaced along the row of coal houses to service every two houses. Drawing water in the wintertime was difficult when the platform would be coated with blue ice and the steps hidden under packed snow.

The coal house was divided in half with two separate doors to service each side of two different houses. A house coal delivery would be designated to the "upper side" or "lower side" as a specific address. Very accurate records were kept by the delivery men due to the aggravation and hard work involved if the coal was put in the wrong side of the coal house.

An honor code emerged concerning the coal houses because keeping the coal house filled was a constant struggle for families. To steal coal from your neighbor was considered a low-life act and looked upon with scorn. A reputation for stealing coal could give your family a bad name. Although rarely a confrontation was seen, a whispered warning was passed to a new neighbor if he moved next door to known coal thieves. The banister meant a clear division of families. The front doors were located next to the banisters, side by side. Just enough space to make lifelong friends or bitter enemies. Families, for better or worse, like a long term marriage, learned to get along.

FRONT PORCHES

Nearly every front porch was graced with a swing, filled on hot summer nights with gossiping women or young folks sparking. Men folk tended to sit on the porch steps smoking, drinking coffee, talking shop, showing their respect for the swing as a woman's domain. Stepping onto a porch meant invading the privacy of a man's home. This right was reserved for insurance men, ministers, church ladies, family members, approved suitors, door-to-salesmen, the likes of the Watkins man, and preacher Bill Browning, who sold Raleigh products on the side, and never forget the dreaded bill collectors.

It was not unusual to see women ironing on their front porch in the summertime. This allowed them to visit with passers-by and helped pass the time for this dreary chore. Items to be starched were dipped in a cooked solution of water and corn starch or flour after their final rinse. The heaviness of the starch made was at the discretion of the wash woman, the heavier the starch the harder the clothes were to iron wrinkle free. The last rinse tub held bluing, a product used to keep your white clothes white. Ironing consumed many long hours standing on your feet. Shirts, pants, dresses, aprons, handkerchiefs and pillow cases were starched and meticulously ironed. Starch-stiffed clothes were sprinkled with water, rolled into tight buns, and kept in towel-lined, wooden bushel baskets. Work to be done was expressed in "how many baskets you had to iron." Starched clothes created a special problem in the summertime as they could sour and mildew in our humid climate if kept too long. Some fussy women had the reputation of ironing their husband's socks and underwear! Stretching curtains and starching doilies were added to the list of necessary chores of a well kept house. Starched lace curtains were stretched on a wooden frame and pinned to a zillion needle-sized pins around the edge. A nimble-fingered woman could make extra money stretching curtains for her neighbors as it was tedious work few women enjoyed. Crochet doilies were starched stiff enough for the frilled edges to stand at attention and that seemed to require a special knack as well. Women would exchange secret recipes for making "the perfect starch" as readily as sharing a recipe for the table. Everyone admired the crisp handiwork showing off the intricate patterns women made and there was much competition amongst the crocheting ladies. Limp doilies were a sign of negligence in a woman's housekeeping. Heaven Forbid!

It seemed to me as a child, the daily goal of most women was to hurry up and get their work done so they could sit on their front porch and watch the traffic go by. The cars were close enough to the porch railing passengers could roll down their car windows, poke out their heads and exchange a few words with the porch occupants. The porch swing became an important asset when courting rituals began for a couple sweet on each other and the girl not allowed to date. Her swain could cruise past her house the entire evening without her parents catching on. A glimpse of her sweetheart was enough to keep the girl's heart pattering wildly while all the boy's spare change was spent filling the gas tank.

A porch swing full of tittering young girls would make it hard to tell which girl was the object of his affection. If the boy pulled a nervy move and stopped with the car motor running he would speak to the best friend, NEVER his love interest. This was the secret code of drive-by dating in the complicated world of romance. The best friend would pass love notes between the two and become the watch guard of the developing affair as she was privy to their feelings for one another. The best friend would guard this trust with her life. However, romantic love can be a fickle emotion so as Grandma Kincer would prophesy, "See two women walking hand-in-hand, you can bet your bottom dollar one has the other one's MAN", was cautionary advice and came in to play when a break-up occurred.

I was NOT standing on Grandma's front porch with my cousins watching on the grim day B.J. Adams' body was brought out of the mines. His widow, Anna, and daughter, Betty Faye, were our next door neighbors for many years after our final move to Haymond. Lives could be changed in an instant in the coal camps with the death angel always hovering near and you could observe it all from the front porch.

BACK PORCHES

Back porches never held the glamour and excitement of the front porch. This is where families continued their daily work. A wash stand holding a basin and shaving mug with an old mirror and towel rack nailed to the back wall was a common sight as the miner liked to tend to his personal grooming at home. The wash tubs were hung on the wall, the washing machine and wash bench crowded the tiny space along with the mop, broom and dustpan. A lightweight clothesline was strung between the posts at the edge of the porch. Sponged-out unmentionables were hung here in the summertime with the kitchen towels. No decent woman wanted her intimate wear exposed publicly hanging on the wash line! If she did use the clothesline, the apparel was discreetly hung between the sheets. In the summertime the wife did her laundry here. I cannot express to you how difficult this chore was for the women. Water had to be carried in from the communal pump and heated on the kitchen stove. Laundry done in an old fashioned wringer Maytag was arduous work. Laundry was wetter and heavier as the clothes were not spun-dried and the wringer jammed constantly. Two rinse tubs were set up so the clothes were put through two rinse waters before meeting the clothesline. Buttons and zippers were broken and chewed up every washday on the journey between the tubs. The wash woman's arms and back ached from handling the heavy wash and her hands turned an angry red. The wire clothesline had to be faithfully cleaned due to the black residue left from oxidation or laundry streaked with black resulted. The laundry was at the mercy of the elements--could be stiffened by winter wind, peppered by coal suet or soaked by a sudden shower. This work was easier in the summertime because the wash was done on the back porch and the water mess was outside. Rinse water was used to scrub down porches and kitchen floor. Carrying water by the bucket teaches you to be resourceful with its use.

Two vivid memories I carry about washing on the back porch at Grandma's have stayed with me through the years. One occurred the day after my oldest brother, Albert, was born, which was also the day following my sixth birthday. My family always stayed with Grandma for the birth of a baby, the tradition started with me and ended with Richard, baby number four. My youngest brother was born on South Fork of the Pound.

How a birthing room was set-up in these cramped quarters remains a mystery to me. Aunt Vestie and her family were living with Grandma which meant a fun time for me to be with my cousins. The company doctor appeared magically and I knew he had my new sibling in the black bag he carried. My brother was born a few minutes past midnight and my father stolidly refused to fudge the time and comply with mother's wishes to give us the same birth date. "Might mean his life some day he was born on this date, Reba." Enough said. My father held a sacred sense about individuality and believed your birth date was your statement of this event.

Next morning, we children came bounding around the corner of the house just in time to see a mountain of snow-white sheets covered with blood being stuffed into the washing machine by Grandma and Aunt Vestie. The crimson red was tied to my brother's birth. I didn't understand how, but I did understand why we children were shooed to the side yard by my aunt. My insides jelloed at the bloody sight knowing it was my mother's blood reflecting the morning sun. Now I understood why she had to stay in bed for days following the birth of my brother where she became paler and weaker, feeding my dark fear maybe she might die.

The other incident is another lesson about minding. My cousins and I were warned to stay off the back porch on wash days and NEVER put your hands near the wringers. This was an open invitation for us to test. The first stolen opportunity, we lined up to hurriedly to run our doll clothes through the wringer. As usual, I was the last in line with enough time to hear my conscience clearly telling me, "NO, NO" but not enough time to stop my hand from slipping between the rubber rollers that quickly swallowed my arm, grinding it up to my shoulder. Midst our screams for help my aunt Vestie came running to release the wringer. I could see the alarm in her face as she was examining my bruised arm. I just knew I would probably lose my arm soon as the agony ceased. I didn't, but my "minding lesson" was painfully learned.

Grandma Kincer

GRANDMA'S MORAL VALUES

Grandma Kincer used storytelling to instill moral values. Grandma was the mother of four children and I never saw her with a man. My grandfather was an apparition who had been gone so long nobody talked about him, including my grandmother. I vaguely knew the story of his early death due to a kidney condition. On rare occasions, Grandma would talk about the terrible time her Alex had. "Why his privates swelled up to the size of a cantaloupe," she would say as she carefully measured an invisible circle in the air with her hands. I always felt grown-up when she shared such intimate details as I never knew quite what we were calculating. My little brothers were my only visual reference which made the story even sadder to me. This is the most graphic talk about sex I ever heard from Grandma. Her modesty was evident as she grappled with ways to share her moral values. Cousin Aggie reminded me of Grandma's reaction to her young granddaughters, Agnes and myself, being exposed to a flasher at the Cincinnati Zoo. "Did he show you his furlough?" she asked us nonchalantly after she heard about the incident, as if we might have seen an ingrown toenail. NOT THAT! We suppressed a giggle. "Oh, Grandma had a way of asking you something and never use a dirty word but you knew what she meant," writes my cousin Agnes.

Grandma liked the idea of her granddaughters being "smart." Smart, to her, had a different connotation than "school smarts." Some of the most worn-out looking women I knew drew her greatest praise. "I declare," she would say in her soft, melodic Kentucky talk, "law, I declare, I don't know how they do it. Why Aunt Polly can break a mess of beans--never leave a string or miss a break between a bean. Her pot of green beans is such a purty sight. Did I mention Aunt Delsie came by yesterday? She's pearter than I've seen her for a long while. Pond my honor, I don't know how she does it with all them boys of hers but her house never has a speck of dust. Why, you could eat off her kitchen floor and never find a dirty dish in HER sink." Aunt Nancy washed the whitest clothes, Aunt Neelie did the finest needlework... on and on she would go, depending on her mood and work schedule. But NONE could compare to Thurston Adams' girls.

My cousins, Eva Dean and Agnes, and I would patiently listen to this round of praise for all these women as we washed and dried the dishes while she put the food away. Not forgetting Grandma's teachings about sweeping the floor and being sure to sweep under corners of the kitchen cabinets. This final step meant the dishes were done. We knew the end of our lesson was coming when she mentioned Thurston Adams' girls.

"You girls are gittin' old enough to commence courtin' right soon. (We would roll our eyes and look at the ceiling behind her back.) I sure hope you will be FINE housekeepers like Thurston's girls," she would say, emphasizing the word "FINE" like it was gilded.

Now, Thurston Adams had inherited a fine farm in a holler in the Cumberland Mountains. He raised his share of corn, wheat and cattle, settling there when he was a young man. He built his bride a four room house and their life together began. Time passed and children were born forcing Thurston to build on to his house until eventually his wife was the mistress of a sizable farm house. Tragedy struck and Thurston's cherished wife died suddenly from an unknown malady. According to Grandma, the love had been so great Thurston could never bring himself to remarry. Somehow I always felt Grandma embellished the story at this point to make housework a more palatable subject. "All he had left to console him were his daughters. Such a pitiful life pore ole Thurston has lived being so lonely and all," her voice would trail off. "MY, but their mother trained them well," Grandma would say in a hallowed tone of voice. Then she would pick up steam and start the praise train, "Pond my honor, I declare them's the hardest working women I know. They cook the finest dinner you ever saw, keep a spotless house, do church work, tend their garden. Law! Their cellar stacked plumb to the rafters with their canning is a sight to see." We would always live the story to this point.

My cousins and I were nearing our teens and we knew these Adam girls to be older women. We also knew they had never been married and were still keeping house for their father. "BUT GRANDMA, if the Adams girls were so smart and handy how come they didn't get married?" we would exclaim in unison. She never seemed to hear that question. We were left with the image of a man living in a perfect world with women doing all the work. Hard as I tried, I could never conjure up much sympathy for this poor, grieving widower, but I never let on to Grandma.

One of my favorite stories she told us when she was in the right mood was about Lucindy who lived way up on Pert Creek, just about the last house before the road ended and backed up against Pine Mountain. Now you have to know, my grandma talked with her hands in motion so you never missed the smallest detail of her story. The minute she put down her paring knife or started drying her hands we knew the show was about to begin. Her eyes would crinkle together and she would smother a grin. Way back then women wore aprons as their carryall as well as a cover-up. A "dandy apron" had many pockets, these mountain women appreciated. These pockets held cracked corn, handy to call their many chickens, seeds from their garden and flower beds they collected while doing their daily work. Maybe a small pair of clippers, scissors, needle and thread like my grandma carried. Grandma taught us to save everything- paper pokes, twine, thread, metal snaps, tacks, nails, wooden spools, stockings with runs, buttons, the elastic, hooks and eyes from old bras and underwear. Anything necessary for an emergency she seemed to find the solution, either in her apron pocket or the big black purse she always carried.

So when she told her granddaughters about Lucindy the story took on a deeper meaning. "Now children, there's a fine line between savin' and being stingy. You don't want nobidy to think porely about you like they do Lucindy." and she would start. "Pond on honor, I declare, that wuz thuh stingiest woman I ever knowed. She wuz tighter'n Dick's hatband. She was so afraid somebidy would take somethin' of her'n, she spent her days looken down the road to see who was coming. Nobidy got passed by her gate thout she crossed them. One of the hottest days ever, why you couldn't even breathe right, hardly any air atall, this pore ole feller came meandering up the road. Lucindy sees him coming." Grandma's eyes widen. And she looks long at each one of us and asks, in a disgusted tone of voice, "Now jest what you think she does???? Why like a mad woman she commences to yank all her shucky beans off'n the porch wall running in the house with them thare strings jist a draggin'. Then she starts puttin her roasn' ears in a big rain barrel sit'n by the porch steps. She had a heap of 'em stacked on the porch cause the corn had just set in." Grandma's arms are flying all over as she is picking up the imaginary ears... "She had her seed beans drying on sheets. Now, here she goes," and Grandma would bend over and grab the sheet by invisible corners and start running across the pretend porch. "Them beans jist a flying everywhere. Her aiming for the front door fast as she could go and the stranger's gettin' closer." We begin to feel Lucinda's frenzy. "Why, Lucindy barely had time to open up them piller slips and shovel them beans in. She almost forgot she had her apron on, and there it was, pond my honor, plumb full of her six week seed beans!" Grandma slaps her thighs. "She runs back in the house and jerks off her apron. Law children, that would have pert nigh kilt her to part with some of her bean seeds." (I should tell you her granddaughters knew how precious seed beans were considered to be and it was a sign of hospitality to share your wealth.) "By the time the pore ole feller got to her gate everything was cleaned off'n that porch slicker 'n whistle, why it wuz empty as a wider's cupboard, it wuz... Nary a thang in sight. Now you knowed how thirsty this pore soul musta been, fer it's a mighty fur piece up to mouth of Pert Creek." Grandma sighed and shook her head knowingly. To offer a stranger food and drink were mandatory rules of gracious etiquette in her times. Travel was difficult in the mountains with our roads so foot traffic was as common as horseback riders and wagons. "Lucindy heads out the gate in a big rush, all out of breath, to greet him jest like she's been expectin a long lost friend."

"Fore he even had time to say his name, Lucindy lit into her tale like a firecracker jist lit. Never even offered him a drink," Grandma stopped, gave us her long look of disapproval we well knew with her eyebrows raised like a big question mark. Grandma continues. "Lucindy says, 'Law have mercy! You'd better git on up the road afore that cloudburst hits'." Grandma's apron goes skyward with a flip and she starts wringing her hands. "Lucindy looks upward." 'Lordy, I ain't seen one that looked this bad in many a yare... Hits gonna be a doozer. I gotta git my wash in afore it strikes.' "Lucindy flounces through the gate thout another word. This pore ole stranger, thirsty as he could be, why it's a wonder he didn't keel over there on the spot, was left flummoxed, scanning a cloudless sky."

To be raised with such clear cut values about honesty, saving, sharing, cleaning, cooking, behaving ladylike and being careful about our choices when choosing a husband, Grandma was confident she had fulfilled her job training us to be women. I must admit most of her advice still holds true

GRANDMA'S STORIES

GRANDMA'S SUPPER

I wish there was some way of writing tastes and smells so you could enjoy Grandma's cooking first-hand but I am going to do my best to give you a sample with my words. I'm not talking about her coffee cakes made with Real Coffee or her fresh-baked loaves of light bread in her warming oven. That was everyday cooking at her house, not ours. I can hear her say, "I declare I don't feel up to it with my rheumatism acting up like it is, but I've got to make Joe Bill a coffee cake, in case he comes in tonight."

"In Case Joe Bill Comes In Tonight" changed over the years. In earlier times, Uncle Joe could be expected to stop in Grandma's kitchen after a graveyard shift in the #2 mines. Then came the long years of waiting for Uncle Joe's safe return from the war--Grandma thinking and worrying about my uncle, the lonely signalman, on a huge Navy warship sailing on foreign ocean waters. HER BABY. No mention was made of his favorite sweet during these years.

Finally, happy times returned and "In Case Joe Bill Comes in tonight," meant a vacation break in the factory work at Baltimore for Uncle Joe. This was a breakaway time to head for the hills of home, Kentucky. Baltimore was Uncle Joe's final stop and he would not return to Kentucky except to pay visits and eat Grandma's coffee cake. Uncle Joe, being her youngest child, was still privileged. I don't think Grandma noticed he was a grown-up with his own family, at least as far as her cooking was concerned. The ritual of making Uncle Joe's coffee cake stretched the length of my childhood and I never once tasted this sacred dessert. I did smell the cake baking many times and watch Grandma take the honey-browned wonder from her big oven. I would inhale the aroma and long to be grownup enough to be invited to eat coffee cake. The time never came and the recipe is now lost. I can still see Grandma pouring left over coffee from the stove top percolator: coffee, black and thick as heated molasses. The coffee has to be just right to please the creator of this specialty. Since my day never came when I tasted the coffee cake, I am left to wonder if I would have really liked it. But that isn't what I set out to tell you about.

This story took place in early spring long before the garden became prolific. This was "fishin' season eatn' time" on South Fork of the Pound River and Grandma was in charge. Grandma's everyday movements in the kitchen constantly tickled your palate. To have her in the confines of my world was pure heaven. She would not be making sweets at our house as I knew the contents of our cupboards. Our mother was not a dessert maker. I was simply happy to watch her fix supper. We had spent the day with barefoot freedom redesigning the freshly plowed garden right up to the edge of the onions, lettuce and mustard green rows. Our appetite was a mighty force to be reckoned with-- whetted by our spring awakening felt in the garden charged by our childhood energy. Grandma understood that.

It wasn't a simple matter to prepare a meal on South Fork. Whether it was breakfast, dinner or supper, the fire had to be started. This meant I could help by bringing in kindling and a bucket of coal. Grandma would start by removing the two stove lids over the firebox and place them on the smooth cast iron cooking surface. Painstakingly, she stacked the skinny sticks in a criss-cross fashion until she filled the cavity. Then, leaning forward, lowering her head, she would eyeball the mound and deftly place wadded newspaper balls in strategic gaps she had made. Reaching for a box of fat kitchen matches on top of the stove with a swift motion of her right hand while she replaced the back burner cover with her left hand, she then struck a match. For a split second a theatrical gaslight glow illuminated the darkness and the phosphorous smell of the freshly-lit match permeated the room. We realized twilight had found us once again and night was close at hand. With great aplomb Grandma walked over to the kitchen table and lit the coal oil lamp from the single fire head still flaming. To witness such power unleashed from a solitary match filled me with fear and respect for its potential.

I was probably at least ten years old before I collected up enough nerve to strike a match and this was under very controlled circumstances I might add. I took a book of pocket matches down to the creek so I would have a ready supply of water in case the world exploded into flames. One can never be too careful when dealing with dangerous stuff. I had grown tired of the taunts of my much braver cousins. Why, they even knew how to light a cigarette and smoke it! Fire starting would not be my forte, I quickly learned as the paper-stemmed matches crumpled one after the other in my hand due to the dampness. I could never a cook a meal if I could not build a fire, simple as that. To start a fire took courage beyond my scope and I am going to be a woman! There is no way out of this fate though my chest is, THANKFULLY, flat a board. I need to pay closer attention to my Grandma at work as she has the reputation of being a great cook. Maybe I could learn to be a good cook and bypass the swelling breasts transformation if I started now. Maybe, just maybe, if I stayed busy this would not happen to me. You see how complicated preparing a meal becomes?

The fire blazed lively and flicked its tongue teasingly out of the opening. Grandma, satisfied the fire seed had taken hold, gave the shovel a hard push down into the coal bucket. She fed the flame food dug from mother earth and waited. A smoldering moment occurred as the fire assimilated the offering and the kerosote-perfumed smoke choked our airways. A burst of bright light shot forth and a crumbling sound heard as the charred wood fell into the recesses of the firebox. Supper-fire was underway! Grandma most likely had an iron skillet of bacon or pork chops frying for the supper centerpiece. I can only remember the smells, a culmination of taste-teasers made by the tantalizing smell of fresh pork cooking co-mingled with the smell of cornbread baking and potatoes frying.

My parents learned lard was bad for your health and switched to Crisco, thanks to a blitz of campaigning by Procter and Gamble. "Vegetable shortening, better for your health" touted the can labels. Grandma was skeptical about this new-fangled notion and lard was this experienced cook's choice.

The time frame following World War Two direct mailing became a powerful tool for advertising in the mountains, probably an unrecognized market before the war. Rural route holders received sample bottles of JOY, a liquid kitchen detergent....a miracle in the dishpan. Try IT! It's free the enclosed circular read. This was a godsend to women who had to heat their dishwater on the stove or keep the side water tank on the stove filled. The water had to be hand drawn and carried from the well to the dry sink or enameled utility table and carried back outside. Many uses were found before the dishwater was thrown over the creek bank. Kitchen counters, stoves, tables were wiped down, maybe a pair of sticky hands about to escape through the side door would be washed in the fast cooling water. Now, miracle of all miracles! No more scummy pots and pans because the dishwater had grown cold. This liquid soap would suds in cold water! Toilet soaps had new names like Lifeboy, Lava and Lux. The familiar bar of homemade lye soap disappeared.

"Take a pound of bone-white margarine wrapped in cellophane, pop the red button included and knead until the color of butter appeared," the instructions read. "Better than Butter" bragged the label. I knew advertising had been carried too far. Being raised on home-churned butter and glasses of buttermilk with golden flecks of real butter floating on top helped me see the wisdom in Grandma preferring lard. Daddy would have a five pond can of lard in the truck bed for her. Trading at the A&P was a necessary stop before heading over the mountain into Virginia. Grandma could not be without her Eight O'clock cup of coffee in the morning. Again, I am getting ahead of my story!

Grandma turns her attention to the side table where two huge stacks of cleaned green onions and a giant bowl of lettuce were waiting. A smidgen later by the Farmer's Almanac, radishes could be added, but not tonight. Spring was just beginning to show her face by allowing the onions and lettuce and mustard to emerge.

The steps taken to bring this bounty to the table required much labor. The onions were wearing their Jacob's coats. Rich green onion blades attached to creamy white bodies hid beneath this overcoat of ruddy red and brown. The brushy feet of the onions held minuscule holdings of grit, as well as the onion blades. The root feet clung tenaciously to the earth and resisted being disturbed. You could tell this by the way bits of rock and dirt clods were clinging to the roots. Lettuce was equally hard to harvest. Each lettuce leaf had curls and creases which trapped soil provided housing for a multitude of garden insects. Grandma would stand at the well bench and draw up water many times and methodically rinse the greens. Draw up a bucket of water, pour over the dishpan, shake the lettuce and onions vigorously, tip the pan to the side of the bench aiming the dirty water toward the woods. This kept the gathering mosquitoes to a minimum. Grandma kept this movement up until she was satisfied not a grain of grit was left. The mark of a lazy cook was to serve a gritty salad and Grandma would never be guilty of that. NO SIREE!

A bucket of potatoes was brought from the dairy and given a light christening of water to remove the loose dirt. The potato eyes were sprouting new eyelashes and the potato skins were beginning to shrivel. This was the last batch of potatoes to be taken from the tater hole dug in the center of the garden.

A tater hole was a time-tested storage trick probably taught to the settlers by the Indians. A huge round hole was dug and lined with tar paper. The potatoes were placed in the dirt bowl and covered with used oil cloth table cloths, old quilts, and canvas tarps for insulation. The grand finale was dirt mounded over the circle, measuring several feet in depth, then covered with tar paper. An opening was made and covered with a tar paper door so the cook could readily reach her stash.

NOW Grandma had the main ingredients ready to start the feast. The stove was beginning to send out warmth knocking the chill from the night air and water began burbling in the Majestic's side tank. Grandma opened the oven door, stuck her hand inside and registered a satisfied expression on her face. She could always tell when the temperature was just right for her baking, whether it was a pan of biscuits, a pone of cornbread or a cake, a skill nearly impossible to master even if you use a thermometer.

Twilight had said goodbye, night settled in and the walls of empty stomachs were beginning to rub together. Grandma knew mealtime must be soon and would say in a soothing tone of voice, "It won't be long now, children. I'll have everything ready by the time your mother finishes her milking." The warm darkness softened our tired limbs and leaded our eyes as we waited.

Grandma reached into the corner cabinet and took out two big cast iron skillets and placed them on the now very hot cooking top. Reaching for the lard can Daddy had opened earlier, Grandma scooped out two wooden spoonfuls for each skillet. The lard was left on the table so she wouldn't have to lift the cumbersome can, Daddy's way of making her work easier. Grandma opened the door that held our mixing bowls and the utensil drawer in one swift motion. She strained and stretched to reach the corn meal and flour sacks on the top shelf along with the salt box, the pepper tin, the soda box and baking powder can. Measuring devices were of little use to Grandma, she could extract the exact amount she needed with her expert hand. Pinch of salt, a scant handful of sugar, baking powder, baking soda or a splash of vanilla flavoring, all kitchen wizardry I believed when I saw finished baked goods in her warming oven. Now she would bring that magic to our house and I was so happy.

She dipped into the corn sack with the cracked coffee cup with a big chip in the rim we used to measure sugar, flour and cornmeal and poured the cornmeal into a bowl-same motions for the flour. A swift addition of soda, baking powder and salt went into the bowl measured by Grandma's fingertips. Two eggs were taken from the everlasting supply in the egg bowl on the counter. The eggs were cracked against the edge of the countertop making a fine line before the egg was opened. I never remember seeing Grandma ever misjudge cracking an egg or separating yolks from the whites.

A jar of whigged milk was brought in from the dairy, a dairymaid's disappointment. The distastefully soured liquid was not drinkable but fine for cooking. The temperature of the milk during the clabbering stage had gone awry and destroyed the bacteria that transformed the clabber into buttermilk. Churns of milk were kept "turning" in the dairy. The cook knew when the milk had thickened to perfection by tilting the churns and judging the golden clabber on the sides of the churn. The cream would gather on top of the milk several inches thick. A trained eye could make a close estimate on the number of pounds of butter that would be made on a churning. Women hated to make a trip to the dairy and find a crock of whigged milk considering the waste and no butter but the hogs loved the treat. Grandma relished "saving" anything so the jar of whigged milk, much to her satisfaction, was put to good use.

The big wooden spoon would fly as Grandma beat the eggs into the thickening batter. She quickly opened the oven door to retrieve her cornbread skillet and poured the sizzling grease into the batter giving the ingredients one final round of beating, then another magical moment, as she sprinkled cornmeal evenly on the bottom of the cast iron skillet. The overpowering aroma made your taste buds stand on end. The thick batter was layered over the browned cornmeal bottom. Opening the oven door, she hurriedly placed the skillet inside so as to not lose any precious heat.

At this point Grandma would dust her hands on her apron and turn to the next task at hand, tending the potatoes. Grandma would wield her paring knife skillfully around the potatoes. They were soon peeled and the shaved bodies given a close inspection to be sure the dimpled eye holes were clean then dunked into a pan of water. One by one Grandma would slice the potato lengthwise into two sections then cut again to make long even slices. She did this without the potato ever leaving her hand and the slices would fall into the water. Occasionally she would stir the water to insure the potatoes did not darken.

The time had arrived.

Grandma would reach into the pan, take a handful of potatoes and shake them vigorously and put them into the emptied cornbread mixing bowl. When the bowl was full Grandma would take her hands and thoroughly mix the potatoes with the leavings in the bowl, coating each slice with the creamy cornbread film. The skillet was filled to the brim and a dusting of salt and pepper added. The searing sound of the hot grease attacking the potatoes was soon replaced by a crackling sound as the potatoes adjusted to the heat, then the steady staccato as the frying set in seriously. Grandma put the lid on the skillet never to be lifted until her keen sense of smell told her the potatoes had browned into a thick crust. She would turn the giant potato cake only once.

Now it was our time.

Without saying a word Grandma would reach into the cupboard and get a saucer. Taking her spatula she would probe gently into the crusty layer and scoop out a few choice potatoes and carry them to the table for us. "Now be careful, children," she warned us, "they are mighty hot"-- a clever cook's way of keeping children from underfoot while she made the final dish.

"Kilt lettuce" it would be as the season was just right. The coffee can of left over bacon grease was poured into a baby iron skillet and placed on the stove. Grandma turned her attention to the side table laden with the freshly cleaned greens and onions. A generous bundle of onions was laid on the cutting board and finely chopped, tops and bottoms. Her paring knife made a few trips through the tender lettuce before Grandma took the palm of her hand and scooped the onions into the bowl and ever so gently mixed the onions through the lettuce with her hands. By now, fine bits of bacon began to spatter on the stove indicating the grease was plenty hot. Grandma remained unperturbed. She had two more acts to perform before she could declare supper was ready.

A big serving bowl was removed from the cupboard. Grandma would quickly run her spatula under the potatoes, each time lifting a scrumptious serving of potatoes and placing it in the bowl. This she put into the warming oven. The smell of cornbread baking had long given way to the richness of the smell of potatoes frying. BUT Grandma had not forgotten her cornbread. Reaching into the oven she found the skillet handle with the well worn hot pad. She lifted the skillet and placed it on the stovetop. The crust was riddled with white seams where the molten treasure had expanded and ridges of burnished veins meandered across the crust. This is not the side for admiring. Grandma quickly flipped the pone to show a proud round of two inch thick cornbread she slid onto the plate. A fine beading of brown lace covered the corn pone, fooling the eye into believing it could be a sweet cake. You couldn't tell the difference.

Now to the salad.

Grandma opened the cider vinegar bottle and poured her magical potion into the hot grease anticipating a mini-explosion. Ever so swiftly she takes the volcanic skillet over to the side table and holds the roiling goods over the salad bowl. The sizzling sound of tender verdant greens and new onions melding into the taste of a new spring is only seconds away from the supper table. I could never eat the entire skillet of potatoes or the pone of cornbread as I envisioned doing while I watched her cook and my hunger was at its highest peak. Only in my dreams can I long for a second try.

Later that spring the Rural Electrification Act from Washington began its mission to electrify our countryside. Lineman from the county cut a swath of trees and underbrush near the South Fork creek for the right of way of the skinny light poles carrying a single wire that changed our world forever. Wood burning cook stoves and cozy kitchens lit by coal oil lamps were gradually replaced by electric stoves and 60-watt bare light bulbs. The memory of Grandma fixing supper was stored in my memory bank so I could share the story with you now.

GRANDMA'S FISHING DAYS ON SOUTH FORK OF THE POUND RIVER

Its early April here in Oregon at Still Point but feels even earlier in terms of spring. I glance around the mountains and note the fresh snow and I feel the refrigerated breeze around my shoulders. The fresh tilled garden is marked with tell tale dents made by the deer, a discouraging sign to see for the eager gardener. I'm down on my hands and knees delicately pulling leeks from a matted clump. "Why leeks won't grow from starts," says my lifelong gardening friend, Stella, emphatically, "you have to plant them from seed." The bundle of brown bulbs hiding in the dirt clod look like green onions sets to me so I will gamble my odds. Ron, our master gardener neighbor, gave me two huge clumps of starts, flower heads from his last year's garden. Early spring always stirs up my memories of Grandma Kincer and her fishing days.

I would wager this was as near a vacation she ever experienced. Apparently, this time of year awakened a deep secret passion inside Grandma which she found too hard to resist-- the irresistible urge to go fishing! That ageless pastime we know can make liars out of most anglers who habitually boast about catching the biggest fish. Of course, our modest grandma was very quiet about her love of fishing so few people knew she suffered from this fever every spring.

Grandma Kincer never spent much time with us in those days because we were living on South Fork of the Pound, more than a mountain away from Haymond. Her visit entailed much preparation for her to be gone so far away from home. I always knew when it was time for her annual fishing visit as the frogs began their incessant croaking. The tiny tree frogs and giant bull frogs in the creek competed for air time. The swampy end of the garden became marshy and filled with gelatinous black-polka dotted globs that clung to dead brush from the past season. Springtime was exciting to me as I would spend countless hours watching the wriggling tadpoles encased in the jelly compartments struggling to free themselves from their glass prison. My unfettered extremities could explore the tadpole environment to my heart's content. Signs of spring were everywhere from the budding pussy willows near the creek to the daffodils pushing through the earth in the flower beds around the house.

Every spring the State Department stocked the creek with rainbow trout in a valiant attempt to restore the balance of nature. Grandma never made her showing until we were certain the big fish tank truck was heard grinding up the road and seen winding around the bend past our house. No attempt was ever made to be friendly to the "wild life men" as somehow their presence reminded everybody of the LAW. The LAW was avoided like a plague whenever possible. Why, rumor had it, you could go to jail if you were caught fishing without a license. It was a new state law meant to limit the catch to protect the streams from being over-fished. My grandmother proved herself to be a very brave woman by posting herself in plain sight of the road where it curved near the creek, as if she were waiting for the "wildlife men" to come by and challenge her right to fish.

Finally, the evening came and Grandma was there with us. She had to wait until Daddy finished his day's work in his truck mines. Dusk would be settling around us and the night sounds starting to sound earnest. Screech owls had begun their nightly forays filling the upper air with their "who-who" cries, whippoorwills were calling "whip poor will, whip poor will" from near the barn and the frogs were croaking frantically around the creek below, that wound its way near our house.

Suddenly, I saw two yellow headlights beaming bright, flickering light off the swiftly moving water in the creek bed. The big yellow Ford truck groaned and creaked its way across the creek and crept up the lane ever so slowly. Closer and closer the truck came toward the house until it came to a squeaking halt at the edge of the yard. Oh I was excited to see Grandma! I could hardly wait for the truck to stop. We had been duly cautioned to do everything possible to make sure Grandma had a good time. She was here! At LAST! I could see two heads bobbing up and down. I was never sure until this moment if Daddy had her because so many people pulled at her time, her fishing trip could be easily postponed. Daddy would always pursue her until she had at least one fishing visit under her belt and that usually took a while considering how busy she was.

Grandma would wait in the truck until Daddy came around to her side and opened her door. She was a short person and in no way could negotiate the high step from the running board to the ground. She would hand Daddy her pocketbook and place her hands on his shoulders and he would lift her out and stand her on the ground. Then she would lean forward into the recesses of the truck floor and retrieve her brown suitcase which she held onto carefully. Daddy would follow suit and reach inside the dark space and bring out the two brown paper pokes Grandma invariably had with her. One poke would have her supply of figure eight twisted tobacco plaits and hard candies, horehound drops and peppermint sticks, wrapped in wax paper. We had the smell memorized. How she could keep from eating her stash was a fathomless mystery to me because she always managed to find a piece of candy when it seemed important.

Somehow the idea of tobacco being a bad thing never crossed our minds as the fresh tobacco smell blended into our sweet thoughts because we knew Grandma would share her goodies with us in her special way. Instinctively, we knew to never acknowledge she had these precious items. It might be days in our child's way of thinking before she shared but Grandma knew the right time to make it a special partaking. The other poke would have things she had gathered in her rounds of visiting relatives. Maybe outfits for my younger brothers from a distant cousin whom they would never meet. Whatever Grandma proffered, my mother, the gracious daughter-in-law accepted. This was the custom of hill families.

Mother always tried to have a special supper to celebrate Grandma's arrival. But as I said, Grandma's visit could be postponed in an eye blink by forces unforeseen by us so we might benefit from several special meals before Grandma appeared. I never knew how my parents worked this one out because cooking was not a happy time for my mother. I do know

Grandma taught my mother to cook so no dish she made could have been a total surprise to Grandma.

This particular visit Daddy was later than usual so the supper hour was past. Poor Grandma, weary from her long day preparing for her visit, only wanted a repast of cornbread and milk and then sleep. What she needed was a refreshing night's sleep and dreaming time. Dreams the fish were bitin', fish bigger than she had ever seen or imagined, hooked on her line waiting for her out there somewhere in the fast rippling waters aiming to strike her line!

Next morning the stage was set. Daddy took a kitchen chair down to the creek side and placed it at the foot of a favorite snag Grandma swore was where the fish stayed. He placed her coffee can spittoon and jug of water nearby. My brothers combed the barn lot for the fattest fishing worms they could find. Grandma appeared in a fresh dress with a newly starched apron. Her legs were encased in beige-colored cotton stockings and her feet protected by prim low-heeled black oxford-tie shoes she always wore. Then she donned one of Daddy's old felt hats and a cast-off long-sleeved shirt of his to complete her sport's attire. Lastly, picking up her can of fresh dug worms, Grandma would round the bend at the garden's edge and dip quickly out of sight, heading for the Henry Hole. Fine fishing soon began!

The swimming hole was fondly called the "Henry Hole", named for some poor soul long forgotten. It was so long ago I don't know if Henry was his given name or surname. In fact, I never heard for certain with my own ears if indeed his lot had been a watery grave at this very spot. If so, maybe this explained some of the wispy figures we thought we saw rise in the mist that rose over the creek late at night. Ghostly sights appeared frequently on hot summer nights and it seemed you could only see them when you wandered, half asleep, outside to the porch, trying to catch a cool breeze made by the creek water fan. We left our private thoughts about this in the night world and never talked about it when daylight came. This secret knowledge was never divulged to Grandma since she never did any night fishing.

Grandma would sit there in her fishing chair until the sun arched high revealing her with its naked heat. Perspiration beaded on her brow and her cheeks flushed, she sat in the merciless sun with no shade. The silence was broken by an occasional gulp from the water jug as Grandma refreshed herself more frequently. Grandma sat there for hours by the creek. If we tried to join her on this venture she would turn her head ever so slightly to acknowledge our presence and in a loud stage whisper would say, "Shhhhhhh, the fish can hear you." Not another word. Fish waiting time weighed heavily on restless young limbs and we would steal away quietly just like she knew we would.

AH, but the by-laws of the art of fishing have inherent rules… sooner or later they bite! Suddenly came the primeval cry of victory! Why we could hear her from the inside the kitchen loud and clear. Racing down to the creek in a discombobulating bumble we witnessed an amazing sight. There stood Grandma with her fishing pole standing beside her and a big grin on her face. Dangling from her fishing line was remarkable golden-colored fish at least twenty inches long. She radiated a victorious glow of a winner. What a divine moment to see our Grandma so ecstatically happy! Funny thing is I don't remember what happened to that fish as my mother cannot stand the smell or taste of Pisces.

coal camp kids

THE TIPPLE PLAYGROUND

Haymond School sat upon the side of the hill, too far away to be our every day play yard. The school yard was small, carved out of the side of the mountain and devoid of playground equipment. We had a far more exciting place to play being near the tipple and railroad. When the tipple quieted for the day, the grounds became ours. The company scale house, run by my Uncle Virgil Kazee and his secretary, Bonnie Kincer(Uncle Fred's daughter), was directly across the road from Grandma's house. Coal gons were weighed there and closely guarded company records kept on the coal shipments. Shelves of ledgers lined the walls of the tiny room. At the end of a workday, the coal gons would stretch out of sight heaped with black gold heading for the big cities.

Near the scale house was a gargantuan covered sandbox, a child's dream. The sand was used to keep the tracks clean and the train wheels rolling on schedule. We considered the sandbox to be ours and played there without supervision. Deep holes were dug and elaborate booby traps were made, filled with broken glass, wire, nails, anything we could find on the tracks. It never occurred to us we were the only victims of our ingenuity. We would build sand castles and forts surrounded by these underground weapons of defense. To our dismay, sand was shoveled daily and would destroy our work but undeterred, we would build again the following day.

Between the sandbox and scale house was the dolly track to take the men to the top of the mountain. The track stopped abruptly on a small incline about ten feet above the railroad track. We had our own roller coaster if we could get enough kids interested in the joyride because we had to push the car up the mountain. Plus we had to trust one of us was strong enough to apply the hand brake, a clumsy wooden handle sticking up out of the right side of the car, otherwise, we could take a deadly plunge onto the railroad track.

One afternoon we had the ultimate thrill as some older kids passed by the sandbox and invited us to take a dolly ride. It seemed easy with them pushing the car to find ourselves higher than we had ever been on the mountain. I looked back down the long track and could see the drop-off and began to feel the adrenalin rush. Straining and giving one final push the assigned brakeman yells "Jump in"' and we went rumbling down the track gathering up speed. The wheels began to click as the car picked up momentum and trees went whizzing by. Our brakeman realized the car was speeding out of control and barked an order for help. We were headed for sheer disaster! One of the boys jumped up, grabbed onto the brake handle with him and they held on for dear life as we careened down the mountain. Sheer fear overtook my senses and I was panic stricken. No one spoke as we clutched the sides of the car and the dolly continued its mad run. The car did not stop until about twenty yards before the end of the track. We could see over the edge of the drop-off. I didn't eat much supper that night.

Eva and Agnes

HAYMOND GRADE SCHOOL

Haymond Grade School sat upon the hill overlooking Bear Holler with its face plumbed to look down toward the complex of the fountain, post office, pool hall, and show hall. The school building clung to the side of the mountain with a steep-graded graveled road leading down to the camp. There was no room for a front lawn, the road ended abruptly and the front steps of the school began.

The road was slick and muddy in the spring, snow-packed and icy in the wintertime. It was a great place for kids to sled which kept the road smooth as an ice rink and equally dangerous to walk on. Grades 1-8 were taught here and then the big move to Fleming-Neon High School was made. I have fewer memories of going to school there than most everybody else because of my years lived on South Fork of the Pound in Virginia.

I did start my school career here when we lived in the original big boarding house in Bear Holler. It was a disastrous beginning. My folks snuck me into the first grade class when I was five thinking I could handle it. I remember standing at the blackboard trying to get my S's turned right and dreading to hear the school bell knowing I would be trampled by the big kids running off the hill. I became terrified on a daily basis so they decided I was too young for school.

I spent fourth grade in Irene Bates' class before my long hiatus to South Fork of the Pound in Virginia. I did not return to Haymond until I was a sophomore in high school and the "Haymond friends" were sophisticated high-schoolers. I am emotionally involved with the school because mother began the long stretch of her teaching career here and the rest of my family graduated from the school.

As a fourth grader, I remember racing off the hill at lunchtime and barely having time to wolf down a peanut butter sandwich before the school bell tolled. Also, I received my first and only paddling from my teacher, Irene Bates. I don't remember the infraction but she went down the row and gave us all a swat on our outstretched hand. That act hurt my feelings to the core, but I still thought she was beautiful and I loved her.

High on the hill, on winter afternoons, when the schoolroom finally became toasty warm, and the fire died down in the pot-bellied stove, this was my favorite time of all. Snowflakes falling lazily past the window, I could see deer feeding near the timberline on the other side of the mountain. The green pines reaching to the top of the ridge with a carpet of white beneath. The valley below was not in sight. My time to dream and let my heart remember these things I see.

Margaret Tolliver, with her beautiful natural curls framing her sweet face, wearing white leather ankle boots with white sheepskin collars she could turn up or down, making the cold winter day seem warmer.

Margaret Trinkle and Peggy Hall with witty smiles and wittier ways, wisely knew our stay on the hill was short and sweet and laughed at life everyday.

I fondly own a "Haymond School" birdhouse, a gift from my dear sister-in-law, Ernestine. When the school was torn down, the wood was used to make birdhouses as mementos, a community endeavor to preserve our memories.

UNCLE FRED KINCER

Mentioning the road leads me to a story about Uncle Fred Kincer. I was always intrigued by Uncle Fred and his brother, Uncle Bryon, since they were my grandfather's brothers. Because I never knew my grandfather I was always hoping they would mention him in their conversation and I wondered if my grandfather would have looked like them. I had never seen a picture of my grandfather.

On the right hand side of the steep road, going up to the school, were two sets of railed wooden steps, about a 100 yards apart. These steps, led to the homes on top of the hill where my great-uncle Fred and Aunt Sally lived. Cap LeMaster's large family lived in the other big house. It was a long climb to reach the top and we cousins dreaded having to be the courier to take messages since we had no telephones. Uncle Fred did! He would make calls for Grandma when necessary.

Uncle Fred's story he loved to tell on us was so embarrassing. Grandma got word Aunt Pearl down on Pine Creek had died. Our mission was to find out if Uncle Fred was going to the funeral and ask if Grandma could get a ride with him. Uncle Fred had a big family and the tailings were two sons near our age, but a bit older. After climbing the zillions of steps up the steep hill, we were greeted by Uncle Fred who was standing on the front porch. He opened the screen door and invited us into the living room full of older boys. We were overcome with shyness seeing all these boys and Uncle Fred pursued us with conversation trying to put us at ease. Cousin Agnes finally got her nerve up and asked the favor for Grandma trying hard to not get twitterpated by the boys. Uncle Fred says, "Why girls, you tell Aunt Ollie, Aunt Pearl is still ALIVE! She ain't dead yet."

A GIANT PAUSE... Not to be outdone and return with a failed mission, quick thinking Aggie blurts out, "Well, Grandma wants to know when she does die, can she get a ride to the funeral with you?" Uncle Fred is probably up there still chuckling.

HEALTH AND WELFARE

DOCTORING

No one can EVER forget the traumatic "shot days" when Dr. Dow Collins and nurse Wells showed up at the school. We were lined up room after room to face the dreaded needle. Tears did not count. Cousin Agnes had the small pox vaccination three years running before the pox finally appeared. She developed a huge painful sore, bigger than anybody had ever seen. It was a long time healing and left her with three concentric rings for a scar.

Doctoring was mostly a home art and few of us saw a doctor or dentist. My trip to the dentist, Dr. Quillen, when I was seven was an emergency with an abscessed molar. My daddy and the dentist were standing together behind the ominous chair. I heard the dentist say, "I'm afraid I have to EXTRACT the tooth." I heard daddy say "OK." The dentist proceeded to pick up his pliers and head for my mouth. My problem was I did not know what the word "EXTRACT" meant. He gave a quick yank which I couldn't possibly have felt since I was already in such pain. I was incensed he did not tell me what he was going to do and I became a screaming banshee. The doctor apologized to daddy for hurting me. I could not explain I was simply furious for not being told what was going to happen to me. Daddy was so bewildered by my outburst and "thought he would never quiet me down, she cut such a shine," I overheard him tell Grandma as I was lying on the bed still snubbing.

Grandma swore by Raleigh's products and made wraps out of woolen scraps for our necks after she slathered us with the mentholated ointment for any head or chest ailment. The ointment came in a round tin with a blue and yellow design. It was good for burns too. Her chewed tobacco poultices for boils and infected sores took care of most health problems in our days before antibiotics. If red streaks developed you were put to bed so infection wouldn't spread to your heart and bring your quick death from blood poisoning, you were told. Dr. Carter had an office in the old boardinghouse and I had my tonsils swabbed with tincture of iodine a few times there, a painful experience. We kids knew sickness and pain went together and expected the sting of alcohol to hurt. Scrapes and cuts were cleaned with alcohol, smeared with "methiolate" and left to heal. Broken bones were addressed by a doctor if a break was obvious, otherwise it was given a chance to heal on its own and pain ignored. A round of worm medicine was given every spring and fall like clockwork. These were the war years and doctors were scarce in our mountains. I doubt I went to see a doctor more than half dozen times in my growing up years. Considering I was a bit on the puny side growing up, I feel fortunate I made it to adulthood.

Coca-Cola earned the name "dope" by the mining communities and was sold ice cold out of the refrigerators at the Fountain. All day long children would be sent to the Fountain to get a "dope" and people became addicted to the drink. "She's going to kill herself drinking them dopes. I hear she is up to six a day," tongue waggers would say, shaking their heads about one of their neighbors. "She's got skinny as a toothpick, won't hardly eat a bite. Why a puff of wind could blow her away." The kick from the drink relieved the tedium of coal camp life for the innocent partakers. Favored soft drinks also included Orange Crush, Pepsi, Dr. Pepper and RC's. Royal Crown Cola had a local bottling plant in Whitesburg and was considered to be our hometown drink. Sweetened iced tea and fresh lemonade graced the Sunday dinner table but coffee was the main drink and consumed by the gallons. I was introduced to coffee at 6 years of age when it warmed my breakfast milk on cold mornings. A lifelong habit began for me; I still take cream in my coffee.

You had to cross the mountain into Virginia to buy alcohol. Letcher County has maintained the status of being a "dry county" which created a thriving business of illegal trafficking of booze through Pound Gap. But that's another story.

Tobacco was enjoyed in every form--smoked in cigarettes, cigars, chewed and dipped as snuff. Cocoa made a fine mimic for the kids to practice spitting. Tobacco could be bought by children at the fountain, meat market and company store so the addictive habit came early.

DISASTERS AND CALAMITIES

The mine was not the only place to meet disaster and experience calamities. The skinny thread of highway running through the camp was a constant source of danger. My oldest and youngest brother both were struck by a vehicle on this road in separate accidents. My youngest brother, G.C., lost control of his bike on the sidewalk and fell into the back bumper of a car driven by a teenager known to be a hot-rodder. The accident was not the teenager's fault but the scare quickened him to become a mature driver. Aunt Vestie witnessed the accident from her front porch and from her angle, it appeared like G.C.'s head went under the back wheel. Tearfully, she told mother to expect the worst but spared her the details she saw. A mad race to the Fleming Clinic, hours later, a frightened, bloody little boy went home with his spliced scalp across the top of his head sewn together, all done without an anesthetic. The doctor was afraid to put him to sleep under the circumstances without an x-ray machine available to assess possible damage. I helped hold his writhing body in place for this procedure with my friend, Dean, who later became his brother-in-law. Albert was more fortunate with his close encounter with the road but he became mindful of the ever present danger.

The other serious accident, which still frightens me to think about, was G.C.'s tumble from the back of a living room chair. Mother moved the living room furniture to the front porch during spring cleaning which meant a new fort for the boy's playtime. My baby brother, G.C., stood up on the back of a chair, lost his balance and fell face down onto the sidewalk, a distance of at least ten feet. He clipped the edge of the sidewalk and his face was pushed in, forming a sunken crease above his eyes. He appeared to have no eyes with the separation caused by the dent and blood was pouring from his face. He was conscious and kept repeating "Don't worry Mother, I'm not going to die, I'm not going to die," as we rushed him to the clinic. Nothing could be done for him except to stop the bleeding and pray. Prayer carried us through the agony of the anxious waiting period. The outcome of that accident is in the annals of the book of grace as his life was spared.

The road curved near the tipple and bridged the tiny creek supported with concrete abutments. This was the scene of many car accidents with speedsters through the years. I remember Bill Collins was killed there one Saturday night leaving his wife, Nancy and young family.

Sometime later, a fuel truck loaded with gasoline, hit the abutment on a hot July day, landed on its side spilling its load into the creek. Within minutes the scene became a live inferno. Gas fumes filled the air as the layer of gasoline rushed down the creek making giant heat devils that skittered atop the water until the moment they froze in space. BOOM! The day, already closed in with oppressing heat, made an inescapable furnace and in a horrifying instant, hundred foot flames swooshed down the creek in a wall of fire. It left the camp with scorched and blistered house fronts and loss of Colis Kincer's grocery store but no casualties-- an unforgettable scene you will always remember, if you witnessed it.

HOME CARE

TB was the scourge of mining communities, the disease that kept everybody fearful. It was not an uncommon sight to see someone wasting away from this affliction. Daddy warned us to not share eating utensils or drinking cups, wash our hands before eating and "don't let anyone cough on you" was his constant reminder. We had our family case, Aunt Maggie. She was the wife of Grandma Kincer's brother, Uncle Will. Poor Aunt Maggie had languished so long bedfast she had lost her voice and talked in a whisper. We would find her in bed propped up with pillows wearing a pale satiny bed jacket, every spit curl in place. We took turns standing by the bedside talking to her. She and Uncle Will were childless so she was delighted to see us even if we couldn't get too close to her. Uncle Will devoted his life to taking care of her and keeping a spotless house. Respectful visits to see her were tedious for children because of the hospital-like setting and it seemed the visits would never end.

Goiters were seen frequently in old people who had bulging necks from the thyroid disease due to the lack of iodine. Introduction of iodized salt and education about the disease has gradually obliterated the problem but Grandma Kincer had this condition.

Then there was Uncle Monroe, Grandma's younger brother who chose to be single for his life. He had the reputation of being a great fiddler and the life of the party in his younger days-- never missed a square dance. He fiddled his life through the lumber camps of Washington and Oregon and never collected himself a wife and family. Advancing age caught up with him and he spent his last years going from household to household to visit. The visit usually turned into a two to three month stay and we cousins dreaded to see him coming. He suffered severely from arthritis and rheumatism which made him cantankerous and short tempered. He spent his days sitting by the fire, waving his cane at us and cursing the air helplessly. This tiny man with a gnarled body, who talked of times we knew nothing about, bossed us around and expected to be waited on. Breakfast time was especially intolerable. Uncle Monroe insisted we children share his special homemade concoction for oatmeal, applesauce mixed with stewed prunes, and we didn't dare protest as we meekly passed our bowls to him. Children were taught to be respectful of their elders. He would heap globs of the god-awful stuff into our oatmeal and watched us with a hawk's eye to see we ate every bite. After this experience, it took me years to appreciate oatmeal for breakfast. I knew he was in pain and God would forgive him for his cursing mouth, but I worried about his contrariness. Uncle Monroe was a "no heller" believing hell was living here on this earth. Considering the torturous pain he constantly lived, he was a missionary of his convictions. His fiddle came to a sad end too. Grandma had it stored in her smokehouse where a roof leak went unnoticed. Uncle Monroe's fiddle came out of its case in several warped pieces one spring cleaning day.

SANITATION

There were more outhouses than main buildings in the camp. Not much thought was given to possible health hazards and I never remember any outbreak of disease blamed on the situation. The biggest problem was the embarrassment suffered by high school girls on honey wagon days. A scheduled run was made by the sanitation department to clean the toilets usually in late summer or early fall. You never knew when your town would be targeted, especially your house. It seemed the honey wagon always managed to be parked in front of my house when the school bus dropped us off in front of the Fountain on muggy hot afternoons. I would pray the honey dippers weren't in my back yard or I would be mortified. The stench was unbearable on torpid afternoons and the football boys in the back of the bus would start catcalling, blaming the smell on somebody. I couldn't wait to get off the bus before anybody noticed where the honey wagon was parked.

THE HAYMOND COMPLEX

Every coal camp was set up in the same fashion. A hub of town business was built by the coal company to meet the needs of the town folk. The buildings--the company store, the recreation center were of the same design, only larger or smaller depending on the size of the mine operation. McRoberts had the popular "Rec Center" which attracted teens from other towns. McRoberts and Jenkins had municipal swimming pools, a great hangout for the young people. Haymond was a minor player on the coal town scene but we had our entertainment center--the fountain, the pool hall, theater plus the post office housed in one building. I would be hard pressed with a pen to describe to you the hustle and bustle lived in this small arena. Our people absorbed the raw and rugged life around them, emerged strong, and now recognize the legacy of the simplistic life they lived.

THE SHOW HALL

The show hall had a separate front entrance on the right hand side of the complex of the fountain, pool hall and post office. Saturday afternoons were spent at the show hall run by the Hampton brothers. We had the opportunity to see two feature films, always a western starring Gene Autry or Roy Rogers and a serious drama. A short comedy usually the Three Stooges and a serial featuring the perils of the jungle or fortune hunters kept us spellbound from week to week. The film would break frequently and the lights would be turned on dispelling the magic and kids would whoop and holler. The instant darkness returned we were transported back into the fantasy of movie land for a dime, places we had never been, but we knew they existed. This movie house had no frills like soft lounge seats or carpeting but always had a packed house.

THE POOL HALL

The entrance to the pool hall was on the right side of the big wooden porch that extended across the front of the building. A long set of cement steps, same length as the porch, led from the sidewalk to the porch. The door to the poolroom was usually open in the summertime so we could sneak a peek inside. The gray clouded room was always crowded with men smoking, shooting pool... and bull. We were cautioned to avert our eyes and NEVER look directly inside. Boys who hung out at the pool hall were NOT good husband material, we were told.

THE FOUNTAIN

The fountain was the front entrance on the porch. Inside you could get a soft drink, listen to the jukebox and meet your friends. The poorly lit room had huge fans constantly moving the air which made it feel cool and inviting in the summer. The oiled wood floor was covered with sawdust. The glass cases were full of candies and cookies which could be bought by the piece. Bologna, cheese, ham, bread, milk, pop and ice cream and cigarettes were carried by the store, our mountain DELI.

THE POST OFFICE

The post office completed this hive of activity for the camp. The entrance was to the left side of the porch and, unlike the pool hall, a door on the other end of the room led to the street. Going to get the mail was a daily social activity and kept everybody updated on the latest gossip as they walked toward the post office. People would start crowding into the tiny room when they saw the wall of glass boxes being stuffed. They knew the postmistress, Irene Mullins, would open the window for general delivery shortly. Letter writing was a serious form of communication since telephones and televisions were scarce. It was especially important to Nina Lee and her friends, Norma and Sarah, to see if Nina had a letter. Keith had graduated and joined the Navy, leaving his heart behind with Nina. We would be so happy to see a letter in Nina's hand!

The Combs family had the ONLY television in our row and it was a big set that dominated a corner in their living room. Mr. Combs also drove a shiny brand new Oldsmobile we girls loved. Our friend, Frances, would invite us in once a week to see the Coca-Cola fifteen minute Hit Parade shows. We would watch our favorite performers like Eddie Fisher on a snowy screen from New York City and be transported to the Big Apple.

The Company Store

THE COMPANY STORE

The company store and meat market were located in the "lower end" of Haymond. The meat market was in a long side building separate from the company store. Here the finest meats were available for a company price and families had a running charge account. The best bologna in the world could be found in Letcher County at the meat market. The butcher would fine slice sandwich meats and cheese in any amount you asked, from a single slice to whatever you needed and add the bill to your charge account. This is where children came in handy as steady runners to the store.

The Company Store catered to the needs of the miner's family. One side of the cavernous space was devoted to groceries, sundries and miner's supplies. Hard hats, carbide for the miner's head lamp, pick axes, shovels, heavy work clothes, thick woolen socks and miner's waterproof boots were available for the miner at a company price. The other side was the department store that carried clothing, shoes and furniture. Furniture was grandly displayed in the store front windows; bedroom and living room sets to tempt the wives to use their scrip money and charge accounts. A poor miner could come home from a hard day in the mine and find the front room full of new furniture that would take him years to pay off.

The wife was in control and could lead her husband to financial ruin if not reined in by the birth of another child or his premature death in the mine. In early days women had this added worry--if a miner was killed his replacement was made quickly as possible and the company house given to the new miner. The homeless widow had to fend for herself best she could. Company debt could be easily equated to home furnishings and grocery buying habits. It was easy to owe your soul to the company store.

I winced with heart pain to see the back page of LIFE magazine showing a full page photo of the row houses in the "lower end" of Haymond. The picture dated to the early 60's, depicting to the country the urgent need for the famed "War on Poverty" campaign our government was waging. I was living in Columbus, Ohio at that time.

LIVING IN A CAMP HOUSE

I don't know why the towns were called camps; perhaps the mountaineers viewed the towns as a temporary blight that would disappear when the coal ran out. The strangers would surely leave. New towns sprung up like wild mushrooms dotting the mountain sides near the coal seams. Towns that were sketched out on the drawing boards of moneyed opportunists living in far away cities like New York, Philadelphia and Pittsburgh. Our coal deposits furnished wealth to their cities and coddled families. Mountain children, like myself, who came of age in the fifties, were well aware of the financial raping our families suffered from the "Big Mines." We were the first generation to grow up in the ghost towns left by the giant reapers.

Haymond was considered to be a lesser mine to the bigger coal deposits being mined in the area. We did not have the big recreation hall, hospital or schools like some of the surrounding towns. We did have two church buildings, one near the tipple, the Free Will Baptist church and the Colored Baptist church, which is no longer there. The Free Will Baptist church has remained a solid pillar for the community shown by the steadfast support of couples like Paul and Josie Richardson and Tom and Irene Edwards.

Haymond Colored Church—1914

Haymond Freewill Baptist Church

Much of my younger life was lived in different row houses where I watched and lived my family's struggles with economics, health issues and the spiritual side of life, a common lot for coal miner's children. I returned to Haymond when I was fourteen years old when my family permanently settled into one of the camp houses.

A coal camp house was a double house made to house two families--a mindless designed shotgun house built with the inner doors lined in a straight row against the inside wall. The houses were built from our then plentiful yellow poplar trees, bought for a pittance from our people.. Timber hurriedly made into green lumber used to construct houses that would settle and warp, leaving gaping air holes around uneven door and windows in the years that followed. The front room had a fireplace with a cement hearth and a rough finished mantelpiece. Two rooms upstairs, three rooms downstairs, half a front porch and back porch, electricity, an outhouse and a small side yard was typical housing for the miner's family.

FAMILY RITUALS

WASH NIGHT

My family felt privileged because we had the luxury of a kitchen sink and running water with this last move. The sink had a chipped porcelain drain board and the water pipe came directly through the wall from the outside. This convenience would make wash night easier for my school teaching mother who had to do laundry after school. Laundry was a family necessity and a job handed down to women of the household. Working feverishly, powered by two cups of strong coffee, mother would set up her laundry station consisting of the wringer washer and two rinse tubs in the middle of the kitchen floor, hoping to finish by early evening. Once I witnessed a discouraging sight for my mother. One of the rinse tubs, sitting on a rickety bench that suddenly collapsed, capsized and water sheeted over the kitchen floor. I stood there feeling helpless, waiting for her reaction not knowing what to expect. She calmly walked over, opened the back door and reached for her mop and broom. Without saying ONE word, she began sweeping water out the open door, an unforgettable scene. My mother will never know how she imprinted me with her sense of perseverance and stoicism.

Our laundry would include at least a dozen pair of jeans for my brothers. The dining room was converted to a drying room and the clothesline zigzagged across the ceiling wrapped around ten penny nails. The Warm Morning stove was loaded with coal and pushed to its outer limit to dry the clothes by morning. Many times I saw the curved stovepipe going into the brick side wall turn a bright cherry red. We lived with this constant fire hazard and by morning the jeans were dried poker- stiff and the house smelled of Clorox and Oxydol detergent, a squeaky clean perfume that kept the house sweet smelling until the next wash night.. only six evenings away.

BATH NIGHT

Bath night started early at our house on Saturday evening. The number 2 washtub used on wash night became our bathtub. The kitchen was setup as a bathroom with stacks of towels on the kitchen chairs surrounding the tub in the middle of the kitchen floor. Water was heated on the kitchen stove and added as needed. My brothers were scrubbed down one by one-made ready for Sunday school the next morning. Ears received special attention as my mother made certain they were scoured inside and out, despite the yowling. Pink-eared and polished clean, my brothers were sent to bed, mother satisfied they were spotless and shiny as new pennies.

Accepting life on its rawest terms was an everyday fact growing up in the Kentucky coalfields. Winters were bitter cold and the summers steamy hot which meant your camp house was either too hot or too cold. Electric cook stoves had replaced wood stoves in the kitchen so the only source of heat was in the dining room with the Warm Morning stove. This was a popular stove in the coal camps because the fire needed to be stoked only twice a day like a furnace.

Burial policies were bought to cover the untimely demise of a child, (God Forbid). This money was hard to come by but it would have been a worse state of affairs with a chronic illness and no health insurance. School clothes were bought on time at Wise's Department store in Neon where the gracious lady, Rose Wise, allowed a charge account. The clothes would be faded and outgrown by the time another round was bought.

Living our lives in this state of grace was taken for granted. The security was provided by the strong faith of our elders who had lived through harder times and could reassure us things could be worse.

Depressing times returned to Haymond when the tipple shut down. Doc Wright, a man of vision, bought up most of the town property from Elk Horn Coal Company. My family rented from Doc Wright who was a benevolent landlord, one who understood when there was no rent money and tenants who expected no property improvements in return. Rent was collected by Doc Wright's bespectacled son-in-law, a tall lanky man, who would show up with his big ledger under his arm and start his walk down the sidewalk knocking on doors. He moved his car at intervals which gave families time gather the rent money or polish their excuse to hold until the next month's call.

Eventually, my family bought the house and owned the ten room house with no bathroom. This happened after I was in college. Our tolerant widower neighbor of many years, Archie Knox, had passed and it seemed the fitting time to buy the house. He was living in the upper side when we became his neighbors and we considered ourselves to be intruders into his space. Young neighbors who brought all the hurly-burley bustle of a growing family he could hear through the dividing wall. Our kind neighbor never once complained about his rambunctious neighbors.

My family moved in and out of Haymond many times as my father would go to the big cities for work. My homesick Virginia born and raised mother tried hard but she could not adjust to Kentucky and coal camp living so she would retreat to the family farm on South Fork in Virginia. She never dreamed this move would be her final stop.

The stark company row houses were gradually bought and changed into single residences. Individuality and pride of ownership began to be expressed. My family home has been modified through the years but the feeling of being a coal miner's home is still there. My sister, Jo and her husband, Doug, have lived in the home since my father passed. Doug worked in deep mining until he retired. On my return visits, deep-seated emotions were triggered by the familiar sight of mining boots parked by the family room door and a lunch bucket on the kitchen counter. The counter would be lined with snacks and treats, rewards for a man willing to risk his life going into the dark caves of the underground. I WAS HOME!

CHANGING TIMES

To set up housekeeping was the expected future for a woman and her hope chest became her dream chest holding her collection of handmade quilts, crochet doilies, tablecloths and dishes. The contents of the dowry box would be discussed among the women in the family if an elusive prospect appeared. Everyone seemed to know exactly what was in the chest so the girl had few private possessions save the sweet nothings her lover whispered in her ear.

The war changed life in the mountains like every place else in the country. Young girls devoted time writing love letters to their sweethearts, waiting for leave time with an expectant heart, hoping to become officially engaged. I was fascinated with the transition I saw girls make in becoming women planning their futures. One lucky girl I knew was given a whole room to hold her dream, a big family sacrifice of space in a company house. My cousins and I were mesmerized by the thought of being in love and getting married. Occasionally the prospective bride would let us see her room that smelled strongly of fresh pine and cedar. The pine bedroom set barely fit into the room with the ornately carved cedar chest squeezed in at the foot of the bed. The cedar chest was filled with beautiful things she was saving for her new home. The furniture was a proud acquisition from the company store where it had been on display for months in the front store window. The debt would be paid off with allotment money by the time his discharge came through she proudly told us as she rearranged the gaudy silk sweetheart pillows he had sent her from Japan, pillows that filled the top half of the bed. Sadly, her lover never returned and she was left with her memories, the silk pillows and his Purple Heart.

Many men returned home in government boxes and given fine military funerals for their heroism. Others were shell-shocked, sick with typhoid fever, unable to work; some brought home war brides to blend into our mountain culture. The period of adjustment returning to everyday life was felt by everyone. Many veterans left to take factory jobs in the big cities like Detroit building cars or went to college on the G.I. Bill and settled in the Blue Grass area. The nation's desperate need for coal, which fueled the war effort, stopped. No more endless orders shipped to the steel mills on demand, we were left with a struggling economy. Education was our only weapon to better ourselves and we inevitably had to go where job security could be found. My generation of the early 50's, flooded the school systems of Ohio and Michigan with educated Kentuckians. I am sure most of them, like me, would have loved to return to the Kentucky home in their dreams.

SURVIVAL

My youngest brother, G.C., commented, "If you can survive growing up in Haymond you can survive anywhere." Roaming the woods around Haymond meant constant danger to my three younger brothers. Mother would say no matter how much blood she saw, long as they were conscious and no bones protruding when they were carried in, she learned not to worry. The doctor could stitch them back together. However, recess at Haymond grade school could be a heart stopper. Mother caught my dare-devil brother Richard swinging from a grapevine on the hillside. She found him suspended mid-air over the valley of Bear Holler, a forty foot drop to the valley floor. He won the bet with his buddies but paid dearly for taking the dare when he got home.

Survival is the life skill you must learn wherever you are raised, be it the city streets or the backwoods of the mountains. The difference, the mountaineer knows, is the mountains and his people will embrace him and protect him when life lets him down. You never become jaded walking up a mountain path or sitting by a babbling brook in a hidden glen claiming the quietness surrounding you while you sort out life's quandaries. A walk down a city street could be your last one if your luck runs out. The mountaineer quickly discerns the difference when he is confronted with city ways. This understanding is your everlasting gift from your mountain heritage to be used wisely outside the hills.

TRADITIONS

QUILTING, WEAVING, DARNING, KNITTING AND SHUCKY BEANS

I can't let my reader go without talking about quilting, weaving, darning, knitting and shucky beans. All five topics are very much a part of molding me into the hearth and home woman I am. Quilting was serious work with women I grew up with. Part of "visiting" would be showing off the latest quilt being pieced. Quilt patterns were exchanged and quilting parties set up to finish quilts in the wintertime. Nearly every house would have a quilting frame set-up, especially if a grandma lived with the family. Every girl had quilts ready for her when she set up housekeeping. My Virginia grandmother, Grandma Adams, made me a "Tree of Paradise" quilt to begin my married life. The solid green trees appliqué against a white background wobbled across my marriage bed in a wavy line because grandma was nearly blind from cataracts, but it never stopped her from quilting. I always felt the warmth of her love when I pulled the forest of paradise trees over me before falling asleep. My mother became a fanatic quilter after her retirement days set in and would quilt herself into a stage of exhaustion trying to catch up for all the quilting days she had missed due to years of teaching school. I know I will never live up to any inherent abilities I might have about becoming a quilter. I have yet to quilt a quilt.

Sarah weaving at Berea College

Weaving is as much a part of my heritage as quilting. I have pieces of linsey woolen woven by my great-grandmother from Cram Creek and her spinning wheel is still in my family. I became an expert weaver when I attended Berea College and earned my tuition weaving. I wove for England's Queen Elizabeth the famous Whig Rose design for her dining room chairs. I don't know which dining room, just look for the Whig Rose pattern the next dinner you attend. I never picked up another shuttle after leaving Berea so I have nothing to show for my skill. The same is true for darning. I was taught in a college classroom how to darn socks though I knew darning was wasting my time. I have never darned another sock in my life!

Grandma Adams also taught me how to knit when I was eight years old. Later, I conquered the art of making argyle socks, baby sweaters and booties. The last time I did any serious knitting was Christmas season 1979 when I made Christmas bell ornaments by the dozen. (My confession here has lifted a ton of guilt from my heart and soul, knowing I will never carry on these traditions.)

...AND SHUCKY BEANS...

Shucky beans remain in my life and mind as a symbolic treasure. I keep some on display in my kitchen. Walking across a plank porch with the back wall lined with drapes of dried shucky beans is a fond Kentucky memory I hold from visits to Pine Creek, along with gourd drinking cups and the water bucket kept near the well. For those of you who have never tasted shucky beans I want to tell you what they are. Green beans (preferably white corn field beans) are picked at their prime, stripped of their strings and threaded into long leis of whole beans. The drying process takes time, depending on the weather. The beans are spread out on old sheets in the sun every day and taken in at night from the dew. The beans start to shrivel and turn brown and they shrink until the hulls rustle like dried corn shucks and are about half their original size--hence the name shucky. Modern day mountain women store them in the freezer at this stage where the beans will keep indefinitely. I will allow a fine Kentucky woman to share her recipe for fixing the beans written in her own words.

Lois Hill-Roy is one of Letcher county's beloved leaders in education. She is known for her work in the Early Childhood program of Head Start. She was left alone as a young widow to support herself and young daughter. She returned to school and has devoted her life to better our future generations. Her husband of many years, Clarence Roy, joins her at the Fleming Head Start program donating his love and time to the children. Lois became part of my family through the marriage of her daughter, Ernestine, to my youngest brother, G.C.

Lois sent me a wonderful surprise of shucky beans for Christmas 2000, knowing I remembered the days of drying shucky beans, how the hollers of Letcher county looked and the ways of fixing "old-timey" food. The inimitable smell of shucky beans and home cured salt pork streaked with dark -brown lean meat stays with me. I could not have been given a finer gift.

A Sun Beam labeled bread bag, chock full of beans with her handwritten note scotch-taped to the side, a jar of grape jelly and salt bacon for the beans emerged from the Christmas box. (I grew up with this happy Sun Beam, a little girl smiling at me from the sides of bakery trucks and light bread bags.) The grape jelly was made from the grapevine in the side yard of my sister's home in Haymond. Mother brought the Concord stock root from her home place on South Fork of the Pound years ago, long before she accepted Haymond was her permanent home. Without further ado its time for Lois to share her receipt;

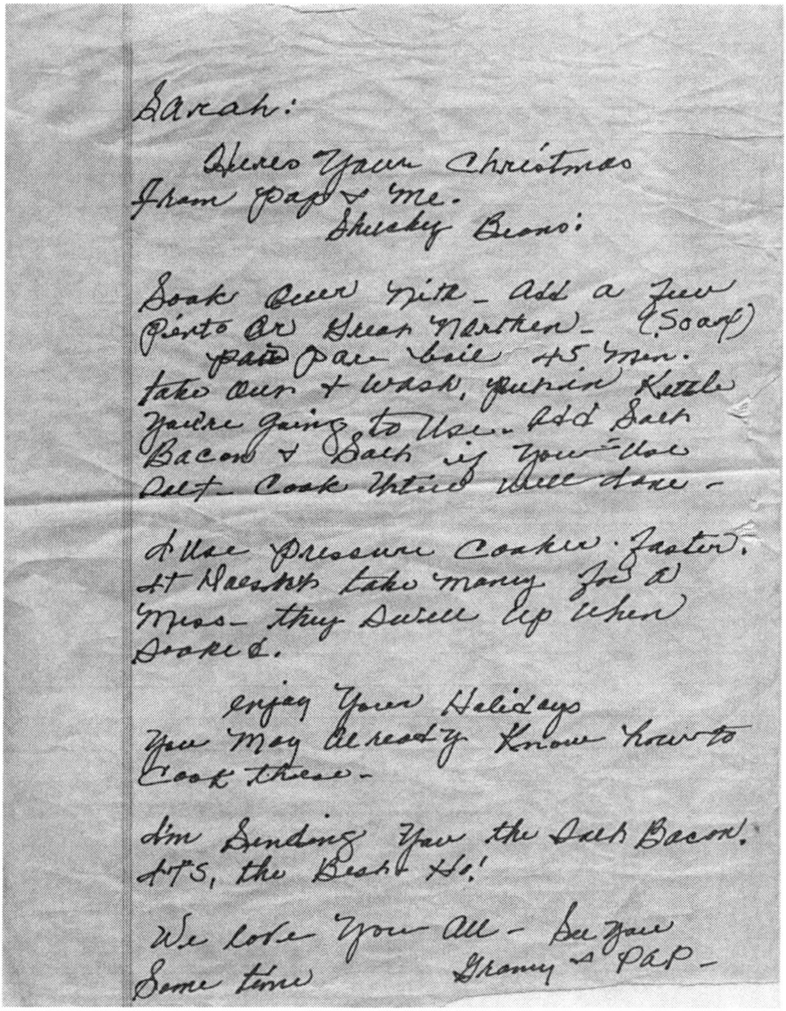

Sarah:

Heres Your Christmas
from Pap & Me.
Shucky Beans:

Soak over nite - add a few
pinto or Great Northern - (soak)
pan par boil 45 min.
take out & wash, put in kettle
you're going to use. Add salt
Bacon & salt if you use
salt - Cook until well done -

I use pressure cooker. Faster.
It doesn't take many for a
mess - they swell up when
soaked.

enjoy your Holidays
You may already know how to
cook these -

I'm sending you the salt bacon.
It's, the best yet!

We love you all - See you
Some time   Granny & PAP -

RECEIPT for Shucky Beans

Lois Hill-Roy

New Year's Eve 1999, I fixed a heritage meal at Still Point, made from my shucky bean gift and my "cornbread" using stone-ground meal (the one tradition I make quite well).

I added a pork roast, fried potatoes and fried cabbage to the table. My Cajun son-in-law, Lloyd, from New Orleans and South Dakota born husband, Warren, were exposed to my mountain version of a "good luck" supper for the coming year.

The New Year's meal was leaner in our camp house. Daddy believed your first supper of the New Year should be indicative of the New Year ahead and be very plain to show your humility and gratitude. Good luck would be with us when we ate the fried cabbage and black-eyed peas along with the cornbread and soup beans. Daddy was trying to teach us to appreciate what we had, knowing this would be the one meal he could be assured his children would be fed and we would never go hungry.

The miner's mainstay served up and down the camp rows was a pot of soup beans cooked with a slab of salt pork, cornbread, kraut, fried potatoes with condiments of hot peppers, and a plate of sliced onions. Fried chicken, chicken and dumplings, pot roast, ham, pork chops or meatloaf were reserved for Sunday dinner in most homes. Possibly the only miner who was short-changed at the table was one whose young bride served him fried burnt bologna and hard eggs fringed with black lace. But he had love and passion as a side dish and was content with his life. Like myself, I am sure people raised in a coal camp think fondly of soup beans and cornbread as being your favorite meal and one you crave from time to time.

LEGACY

DADDY'S BANJO

I know I am a Kentuckian when family stories start layering over one another making it important to find the seeds of truth before folklore sets in. Such is the story of Daddy's Banjo...

I had no idea when I began writing my book that the legacy of Daddy's Banjo would become a wellspring of living truth. On the other hand, I should have recognized this could happen as life is always deeper than it appears on the surface. We are allowed to work our personal history into a private book designed so the owner can handle the pages of harsh truth about life and perhaps himself. What is left of our short stay on earth is our birth date (a figure that could be jimmied) and the more definitive date of departure, which is publicly recorded. Your name, date of birth, date of death, marriages, divorces and birth of children are your legal markers, the only trail we leave behind, regardless of our rank in life or our inflated egos.

How I accidentally met a young writer from the Knoxville News-Sentinel in Letcher County helped me to understand how the ironies in life unveil our authentic selves and possibly reveal our hidden purpose. The young man's keen interest in traditional music led him to Whitesburg, Kentucky, and the Appalshop (National Endowment For The Arts) where our mountain ways and music have been documented and recorded since the sixties. I happened to be there. He was interested in tracking the story of Dock Boggs' banjo, not the musician. He could not believe his good fortune making instant contact with someone who could hasten his search. He was quick to see the heartbeat of the banjo lies in the stories from the mountain people, especially those people from Haymond and Pine Creek. What better place to begin his search? Our serendipitous encounter led to a relationship which was brief but rewarding for me. Being young and curious about life, I am sure he has gone on to more exciting things to write about. For me, I am left to chronicle my personal chapter of Kentucky history.

In the summer of 1981 I was visiting my daughter, Laura, who was attending Berea College in Berea, Kentucky. I walked past a music store on Main Street where a record display in the window stopped me in my tracks. Several album covers displayed were showing Dock Boggs and a picture of him holding Daddy's Banjo. My reflection exposed my wounded heart to me when I looked at my expression in the window glass. I startled myself seeing such deep sadness and wanted to deny the woman was me. I went inside and quietly bought the record collection made by Folkways Recording Studio. This was the lowest point in my life as I was coping with the tragic losses of my husband, Dean, and Daddy, both gone within an 18 month period. This long season of mourning left me bereft, floundering with an empty heart and the crushing blow of identity loss. Buying the albums comforted me and gave me something concrete to take back to my California home but I knew I was collecting memories. Daddy's Banjo was gone. The banjo that was as much a part of him as his coffee cup, cigarettes and khaki work clothes was no longer was in Letcher County.

I recall coming home from California and learning what happened to his banjo. Revival of interest in Dock Boggs was well under way. I could tell Daddy had mixed emotions about letting the banjo go, as he began explaining to me what happened. I was heartbroken for him because I knew how much he loved the instrument. His banjo was his comfort and best friend he turned to in jubilant and dark times. Happy times meant light-hearted songs like "Here old Rattler Here" or "My Old Kentucky Home" while in somber moments he would play and sing "When My Blue Moon Turns To Gold Again." My sister and brothers were roused from bed on school days with the revelry call of "Here Old Rattler Here" in the days after I left home. Their memories, like mine, always include the Banjo.

I thought more about the lonely man who worked for many years at the Radford Army Ammunition Plant in Radford, Virginia. Daddy was a three hundred fifty mile round-trip hard driving away from home with only his Banjo to keep him tied to his home and family. Many times he made the long journey over a weekend to check on us to be assured we were safe. You cannot be raised with that sound without your spirit being indelibly marked and your heart knows you belong to these strings. My Daddy and his Banjo gave us that legacy.

I'm sure Dock Boggs never imagined he would become part of national movement honoring country blues music and return to our doorstep as a folklore hero. Dock Boggs, a country gentleman, was a modest, humble man as was my father. My father's reputation set him apart as a well-loved respected man who had a deep abiding faith in humanity, his church and family.

Daddy's relationship with Dock Boggs goes back to when he was a young man, before his marriage and children. Dock Boggs was at least ten years older than my father so Dock was his mentor, teaching Daddy how to play the banjo in Dock's uniquely original style. When the young man took a wife, Dock Boggs and his wife Sarah rented two rooms upstairs to the young couple with a baby (me). Mother taught her first year of school in Kentucky and Sarah Boggs cared for the infant. Sarah was barren and yearned to have a child and wanted to adopt me. Mother says, "She was such a sweet woman I would have done anything for her. She loved you so much and took such good care of you, made you baby clothes and treated you as her very own. When she asked if she could have you I wanted to cry with her when I said, Oh, Sarah, I couldn't do that. I'd give you anything else I have, but I can't give you my baby." I have known a lot of love.

Dock hocked his banjo to Daddy when Daddy was a young man of twenty, three years before my birth and his responsibilities as a married man. Dock's life became troubled due to his hard living and Sarah, his wife, made it clear to him things had to change if he expected her to stay with him. He gave up liquor and his music to follow the rules of the church and keep his marriage. My family grew up with Daddy's Banjo and never associated the instrument with Dock Boggs as we only knew him through Daddy's stories.

Dock Boggs returned to ask for the banjo over twenty five years later. I will have to tell you this part of the story through the eyes of my brother, G. C., who was in high school at that time. He saw a fancy strange car parked in front of the house so he snuck through the back door to avoid the company because he was coming home from a late football practice and was wearing his uniform. He could hear the men talking in the living room and Daddy called him in to meet Dock Boggs. G.C. does not remember the names of the two men with Dock but my brothers witnessed the transaction. The banjo is something we never talk about because Daddy used the banjo to teach his sons what he valued as the most important lesson in life. "Nothing is more important to consider than the worth of a man's word."

So mountain man to mountain man, within the walls of our humble coal camp home, their code of mountain honor was revealed in front of strangers. The newcomers witnessed something I doubt few men outside our hills would fully understand. Daddy gave his priceless banjo back to Dock for the few dollars Dock had hocked it for years before. They behaved as if the dealing occurred yesterday, not the time gap of more than a quarter of a century. Daddy weighed his decision carefully and knew the intrinsic lesson of the transaction for his three sons was to become "men of their word."

Dock went the route of renowned folk festivals--playing at Newport Folk Festival, University of Massachusetts, Walker Art Center in Minneapolis to name a couple of places--nurtured by the people who had rediscovered him. He enjoyed recognition for his contribution to the music world and his last years on earth.

Time has passed since Dock's death and he is honored annually at the Dock Boggs Festival in Wise, Virginia. To my knowledge, Mike Seeger still has Daddy's Banjo. He shared the banjo with fans at the Dock Boggs Festival in the late 90's. Brother G. C. met him there and Mr. Seeger gave him his phone number and home address so we know where the banjo was at that time.

The last Friday in October, year 2000, Mr. Seeger appeared at the Ginger Rogers Theater in Medford, Oregon. He was on a Retrograss concert tour with his cohorts, David Grisham and John Hartford. The evening of the concert Mr. Seeger was busy arranging his CD's in the lobby of the theater before his performance when I slipped a note into his hand. He took the note and with a perfunctory smile stuffed the note into his pocket.

My note said,

Mr. Seeger,

There is a Kentuckian in your audience tonight who would like very much to meet you and visit. I am a native of Letcher County, the daughter of Garnard Kincer, who gave his banjo to Dock Boggs so he could make his comeback. I understand you are the caretaker of my family legacy. I have had your address for several years but I have been too emotional to write.

Sarah Hagen

Mr. Seeger did acknowledge off-handedly from the stage he had a note from a woman in the audience whose family kept Dock Boggs banjo "for twenty four years or so" and he proceeded to play a piece in the Dock Boggs style. He did not make an effort to contact me after the show so I feel I am being guided to tell the real story of Daddy's Banjo. It is rumored Mr. Seeger plans to give the banjo to the Smithsonian Institute. If so, the history of Letcher County and my family need to go with the banjo. I wanted my reader to know the true Letcher County story of Dock Boggs' banjo written directly from the Kincer family.

This daughter learned the lesson as well as her brothers about being a woman worthy of her own word.

DADDY'S DAUGHTER

Truth cannot be tarnished-
Although it may be hidden by layers of man's indiscretions,
Burnished truth is one of the most powerful discoveries we can find for ourselves.

Sarah and "Strayla" at Still Point

LET ME

LET ME
Stand firmly on this ground
named Still Point,
where winds blow free
and the sun rises at its appointed hour.
LET ME
Face north, south,
east and west,
to survey my domain-
a place of freedom for my thoughts, speech
and secret desires.
LET ME
Embrace all that is mine
in this place,
I call
HOME.

EPILOGUE

Pilot Rock, the vestige of an ancient volcano, is within my sight at Still Point. The vent plug is a distinctive landmark and one I can recognize as far away as Weed, California. The instant I see the familiar lumpy shape in the distance, the feeling of coming home instantly rises in my chest. In inclement weather, the rock will be shrouded from sight and my heart feels the elements pounding on the stone. My inner spirit depends so much on the constancy of this giant being part of my everyday life. When she is dressed in a snow wrap sparkling in the winter sun, I am in awe of her power and beauty. She is presently preparing for her winter dress and her body is wearing bands of autumn hues. I can't see the color bands from Still Point but I saw them on our way back from California last Sunday. Most of the year our lady is a smoky gray color which turns a light purplish haze in the late day sun. Clouds, made of colors of the seasons may waft around her, sometimes hiding her misshaped form from sight. The stone face of "Sarah's Rock", as I like to think of her, has watched me kindly through the years at Still Point giving me reason to believe in much I cannot see. "Sarah's Rock" is living grace.

My Still Point within begins and ends with me.

The seeds of my life have been scattered but not lost. Instead, miraculously, they have been gathered, replanted and nurtured to bloom anew. The form has changed but the harvest promises to be fruitful--gifts from my soul passed to another generation.

Sarah's (Pilot) Rock

ABOUT THE AUTHOR

Sarah Cornett-Hagen, a Kentucky native, lives quietly in the countryside of southern Oregon.

Her beloved home, Still Point, is the touchstone for her lush poetry and homespun philosophical writing. Sarah's sensitive eye for observing patterns of life becomes obvious to the reader as she weaves her magical spell of wonder by sharing her innermost thoughts about life as she lives it. Her most recent published work is found in the anthology, "Poetry as Prayer: Appalachian Women Speak" by Wind. Her tribute to Mt. Ashland, "Mountain Lady" will be published in "The Rag", Albuquerque, New Mexico, August 2004. "Blackberry Heaven" published in the International Library of Poetry 2003, "Colors of Life", captures the essence of Sarah's uplifting spirit.

LaVergne, TN USA
24 April 2010
180360LV00004B/5/P

9 781418 490539